A Catholic Mother
Looks At The Gay Child

Other Titles From New Falcon Publications

A Catholic Mother Looks At The Gay Child

Jesse Davis

NEW FALCON PUBLICATIONS
TEMPE, ARIZONA, U.S.A.

International Standard Book Number: 1-56184-126-9
Library of Congress Catalog Card Number: 97-65810

First Edition 1997

Cover Art by Denise Cuttitta

The paper used in this publication meets the minimum requirements of the American National Standard for Permanence of Paper for Printed Library Materials Z39.48-1984

Address all inquiries to:
NEW FALCON PUBLICATIONS
1739 East Broadway Road Suite 1-277
Tempe, AZ 85282 U.S.A.
(or)
1209 South Casino Center
Las Vegas, NV 89104 U.S.A.

To Brent and Chris

ACKNOWLEDGMENTS

I would like to thank my long-suffering husband for putting up with me during the long hours into the night when he had to endure the incessant noise of the printer. I would like to thank also my best friend, Ethel, for endless hours of proofreading. Their inspiration and support was invaluable.

TABLE OF CONTENTS

Real Life Stories — Case Histories

PROLOGUE

This book should have been written thousands of years ago. Maybe about the time of Noah and the flood. It should have been accompanied by an instruction book: How To Recognize Homosexuality In A Child. How To Tell If Your Child Is Homosexual. Statistics show that 10% of the population is homosexual. This is something that most people in the world are not aware of. This 10% of the population is not just a number in a graph. They come into this world as infants. Born to everyday moms and dads. They go to school, grow up, play, etc. just like everybody else in the world. They don't have to deal with what they are until they get to young adulthood. Then they are in a "no-man's land." No help, no understanding, no acceptance. This book hopes to shed some light on the subject and give some hope to these lonely, perplexed kids. And, in the process, gain some understanding about this subject. This is not a subject that is discussed openly or freely. Rarely is it discussed in front of children, as parents shield their children from subjects that they deem inappropriate for them. However, 10% of these children are living the reality of being the subject of this forbidden issue. This book is especially for them. It is written by a layman for laymen. This author does not pretend to be either a scholar or a theologian. This author has hope in GOD's Divine Mercy for the millions of souls from the beginning of time, 'til the end of time, whose plight this work addresses.

AN APOLOGY TO
LESBIAN DAUGHTERS

I shall take time here to extend an apology. This book does not intend to leave out Lesbian daughters as it is meant every bit as much for them. The fact is that my child is male. My only siblings were male, and four of my five, living children are male. Therefore, I am more familiar with the male child. And feel that I understand them pretty well. I will interview the girls and present their point of view later in my book. Not having a lesbian daughter, I have not experienced their unique set of circumstances. Therefore, I will not try to speak for them, but will let them speak for themselves. I do feel that, even though their problems will be slightly different, their situations will be similar to that of the boys. Everything that I write in this book is meant to apply to them and their families as well. So, that having been said, I make my apologies to the girls and beg their indulgence. When I talk about the boys, I mean the girls and the boys. The important thing is that they are our children, and we love them.

CHAPTER ONE

THE BEGINNING: FINDING OUT

What would you do if your son or daughter walked into your home today and told you that they had something very difficult to discuss with you? You find a private place that you two can talk. They sit you down, and then they say, "I am a Homosexual." I have known this since my earliest childhood memories. I have kept it a secret until today. Now, I have to talk to someone about it. You are my parent. Tell me, what is to become of me? What should I do? How can I live a life just like everyone else? Why did God make me this way? Why am I not like everyone else in the family? Why am I different? How would you answer your very own son or daughter? If they came to you with this reality in their life, what would you say to them? What would you do about it? How would you cope with the fact once you found out? Don't ever say, "It couldn't happen to me." Because you will never expect it, until it does come into your life. It might not be your very own son or daughter. It might be one of your nieces or nephews or grandchildren. It might happen to one of your friend's children, or maybe a co-worker or neighbor. In your lifetime it would be most unusual if you never encountered anyone on a personal basis. Let's just pretend, for now, that it is your own child...

What would you do?... How would you cope with the fact, once you did find out?... Since homosexuals have been around from the beginning of recorded history — Back to Noah and the Ark! — I wonder what parents of that time did? Probably the same things that parents of today do. Grieve over it... Stress about it... Cry a lot... Pray... Worry...

With the statistics showing 10% or more of the population being homosexual, that's an awful lot of stressed parents, and a lot of worried apprehensive kids. The issue, I'm sure, was swept under the carpet, just like it is today. Children, I imagine, kept it to themselves. Just like they do today. Later in life, when they were grown and on their own, I'm sure they lived their lives as privately and as secretly as they possibly could. An entire segment of the population has always had to exist in this no-man's land. I may be thousands of years late with the writing of this book, but...better late than never has always been one of my mottoes. I would like to hold up a candle to this issue and, perhaps, get people to take a new look at this whole thing. I have been looking at it for three years now and I think I have learned a lot. I feel that the world knows next to nothing about this subject. I personally knew less than nothing. I had always been a homophobic. I didn't know any "Gay" people and, what's more, I didn't want to know any "Gay" people. Whenever I noticed them out in public, I just looked the other way. When you do see a homosexual person, it's always an adult. The kids stay pretty much in the closet until they reach adulthood. That's the way it was in our family. As unique as I felt my situation was, I find it was pretty typical of other families experiences. How each family reacts is as individual as all people are. Here is our story.

Three years ago my youngest child, a boy of sixteen, became reserved and quiet. Not his usual sunny, enthusiastic, friendly self. After much cajoling, the most I could get out of him was that he had some deep dark secret that he could not talk about. I remember making jokes. What did he do?... Steal candy from a baby?... Rob a bank?... After all this was my kid. We could always talk about everything. We were always talking. We laughed and joked a lot. He was a great kid. Easy going personality, always up — and cheerful. He liked school. He liked his teachers. He got good grades. He attended a Catholic Prep school. His teachers liked him and he had lots of friends. What could possibly be wrong?... As an elective he was in the drama class and always had a part in the current drama production. Along with his other college preparatory work and busy social life he didn't have time to have a problem. Every time I asked him if he wanted to talk about it he just quietly walked away...

I followed him... "Come on, son! You know you can always talk to me — about anything. I'm a very understanding person." As I look back on it...I remember saying to him, "About the only thing in the world that I couldn't handle, or couldn't understand, is if one of my sons, [I have four], were to tell me that they were a homosexual." I continued, "That is probably the only thing that you could ever say to me that I couldn't handle. But, of course, we have nothing to worry about on that subject." He didn't answer... He just walked into his room and closed the door. I was very perplexed. What could be bothering him? ... I asked everyone that he knew if they could shed some light on the mystery. I found that he had confided in two people. His brother's girlfriend and the girlfriend of his brother's best friend. Neither one of them would tell me what it was.

My question remained the same. What could possibly be so bad that he could not tell me about it? Every time I stated that Homosexuality would be the only thing I couldn't take, I began to notice that there was no reassuring denial. I started to get a sinking feeling. If he's not denying it... Could it possibly mean that it might be true?

Finally, I confronted him...
ARE YOU GAY?
His answer. **YES!!**
It was *true.*

My entire world — as I perceived it — up to that point in my life — crumbled before my very eyes. I spent the rest of the day shedding buckets of tears. How could this be possible?...What could have gone wrong?... What did I do wrong?... I was a failure as a parent... Then panic set in. I had to get him turned around before this idea got too entrenched in his mind. There had to be a way to cure him. When he was a little boy of eight, he had gone through a prolonged period of recurring nightmares. He would leap from bed in a kind of dream state screaming and crying and running through the house. His father and I would catch him and hold him in our arms, and wipe his face with a wet cloth, and talk to him until we could rouse him. Sometimes it would take five or ten minutes to get him out of a dream state into a waking state. All of the time he could talk to us, but nothing made any sense until he came out of it. These dreams were inhabited by monsters right out of science fiction. He became convinced that these monsters could somehow *get him* in real life. All of my reassurances that they were only dreams, and dreams can't hurt you, fell on deaf ears. We took him to a psychologist to help him get over them which, in time, he did. We now took him back to the same Doctor to see if, once more, he could be helped. He saw him about three times and did verify, that in his opinion, our son was a true orientation homosexual. He could continue to see him but didn't think that there was anything that he could do to change what was a reality. I felt that it was very strange that he had not picked up on this situation when he had treated Brent years ago. He had, of course, noticed, as I and everyone else who knew Brent had noticed, that he was not a rough and tumble boy. He was gentle and kind and did not like to join in the usual boy games. He did play soccer and loved track, but he would rather play dodge-ball and hopscotch and talk to the girls. He found them more interesting and better conversationalists. When he was small, at least until the age of five or six, he liked to play with "Strawberry Shortcake" dolls and "My Little Pony" figurines. He considered them his little friends. They contained both boy and girl figures. Even though his brothers teased him about them, I did not think anything wrong. I was relieved however when the movie *Star Wars* came out and his attentions switched to *Star Wars* figurines, and others such as He-Man. At least they seemed more appropriate for a boy. And his brothers stopped teasing him for playing with girl's toys... Well, the Psychologist was a dead end... What to do next?...

My best friend told me of a missionary priest who was doing a lecture series at a local parish. Ironically, it was for families in crisis. We certainly fell into that category. We had a real crisis on our hands. The priest lived about 50 miles from our home. We told the family that we were spending an evening alone and we drove out to see him. Of course, we couldn't discuss this with anyone in the family. Who could possibly understand? We had to keep this to ourselves until we could work out a solution. The missionary priest confused us further by telling us to just accept our son for what he was. He told us to love him and be supportive of him. He also told us that he had a Gay couple on his counseling team, and that as far as he was concerned, they were just as married as any other couple... My husband and I drove home shaking our heads.

Surely this guy couldn't be a real Catholic priest. There must be some mistake. Now what?... Where to turn next!... What to do?...

The high school my son attended was headed by a principal who is a marvelous priest. He loves kids and really understands them. We made an appointment to see him. He comforted and sympathized with us. He also recommended a good counselor. He suggested that we try to keep our son very involved in school activities. We went home and tried to get through one day at a time. On the home front my daughter and daughter-in-law speculated on why Mom seemed to be so upset.

Brent started coming apart at school. He was being roughed up by the guys. Teachers and counselors began looking at him as an unwelcome problem that they didn't care to deal with on a Catholic campus. A gay kid isn't made to feel welcome anywhere. Not by his parents, not by his siblings, not by his teachers, not by the other students, not by his friends. Coming out is an extremely lonely time of rejection. At any age this would be difficult; at sixteen it has to be very scary. Needless to say, he spent a lot of time sitting in his car alone, crying.

He was losing heart and losing interest in everything that had been normal in his life. We managed to keep him in school until Christmas break. At the same time we grounded him. We kept him a virtual prisoner at home because we were afraid to let him out of our sight. Maybe something sinister and terrible might happen to him. We even followed him around to make sure that he didn't fall in with any "strange Gay" people.

Counseling began with a female Psychologist. I gave her a laundry list of my goals.

This is my money I'm spending here.

This is what I want to buy with my money:

1. *Fix Him.*
2. *Turn him back into a heterosexual.* (I have to state at this point, I did not realize that he had been a homosexual since birth and, therefore, could not be turned "back" into something that he wasn't, to begin with.)

3. *Hypnotize him.* Find out where things got off track.
4. *Get him to go out with girls.*
5. *Get him sexual experience. Hire a hooker!!* (I was desperate. This is against my moral code. I had a hard time with it.) My secular side said, "It's the only way to show him that he is really OK and can get married some day and live a life according to God's Laws." The Catholic side of me said, "How can you even consider the commission of a mortal sin? A sin is intrinsically evil and cannot justify a good." This whole issue never got past the internal argument I kept pro-ing and con-ing in my own mind.
6. *Turn him back into the wonderful-amiable-cheerful-witty-fun-loving-outgoing kid I've known all his life.*

We even considered taking him to Ireland, placing him in a seminary, and letting the priests finish raising him. Those Irish priests really seem to have a wonderful grip on life. I was sure that they could help him. How to get him on an airplane and into the seminary was going to be a problem. BUT... We could work that out somehow...

She listened patiently to all of this and then proceeded to chit chat with us as if I had said nothing.

How did I feel toward my son? How did his father feel about him? What kind of childhood had *we* experienced? How did we relate to our parents? And *vice-versa?* She asked us to come back as a trio, to encourage Brent in his school work, and to set up some rules for him to live by: curfew, chores, bedtime, etc.

At later sessions she covered how Brent felt about us-about school-about his brothers and sister. How did he feel about himself? What were his goals in life? She started to see Brent also by himself.

It was at these sessions that I told myself she was "fixing" him. After six or so visits, I restated my list and inquired about her progress...

She looked me firmly in the eye and said, "Mrs. Davis, if you follow this line of thinking and this approach of dealing with the issue — **YOU ARE GOING TO LOSE YOUR SON.**" She held the gaze during a long silence — I guess to let this fact sink in.

Then she continued... "He will pull away from you!... He will move away from home as soon as the opportunity presents itself!... He will live his life apart from you!..."

"Is This What You Want?..."

Of course, it wasn't what I wanted. I love my son dearly. We had always been close. We were good friends. We did a lot of things together and confided in each other. WE WERE BONDED...

From this point on I went into a holding pattern. There wasn't going to be any quick fix. In fact, there wasn't going to be anything that I, personally, could do to change the situation.

I needed to get a grip on myself. Stop stressing. Get back to the business of living a life.

I still had one more path to take and that, of course, is the most important one of all to consider. And that is...

GOD HIMSELF... I had been praying and going to daily mass and making novenas all through this. Up to this point I had been asking God to do something. I wanted him to take it all away. I needed answers. I at least wanted a game plan.

I felt a need to do something positive. I started a prayer support group for parents of gay children...

I knew that there had to be other parents out there just like ourselves, groping in the dark, searching for answers. We needed help. I ran an ad in a local Catholic newspaper. I felt better. At least I was doing something...

CHAPTER TWO

SOURCE:
HOW DID IT HAPPEN?

With the prayer support group under way, I settled in to look for some answers. I found a lot of parents out there going through the same things. I kept getting the same story over and over again. An average family, an average lifestyle, heterosexual (straight) brothers and sisters, and out of the blue, a gay child. All of the parents had the same feelings. They are completely in the dark as to how it had happened and all wondered if somehow it could have been their fault. They raised their children in the same families, in the same manner, with the same values. How can one child turn out differently? I found a lot of pain out there. So much uncertainty. No answers. No solutions. Only questions. There is only one Person that you can turn to. And that Person is GOD HIMSELF.

My thought processes started leading me down a path... I reasoned and reasoned. I prayed and prayed. Certain facts started to emerge...

GOD CREATED BRENT

God had somehow allowed Brent to become a Homosexual. He has been what he is since birth.

— It might be genetic.
— It might be some hormonal defect.
— It may have been some unknown factor that happened to him during his childhood.
— No matter what happened — something did happen — He is what he is.

GOD PERMITTED IT TO HAPPEN

This realization was like running into a **BRICK WALL**. This is a great, *Big,* Giant fact that every person in the world who has a negative attitude toward Homosexuals needs to face, and ponder.

So, even if something happened to him that we were unaware of during his childhood or growing up process, something that could have caused this to happen, it still happened with God's permission. Remember, JESUS said, "A bird does not even fall out of the sky without the permission of OUR HEAVENLY FATHER." Therefore, God must have some reason behind the fact that Brent is a homosexual. Being a mere mortal, there is no way that I, or anyone, can discern the MIND or thoughts of OUR CREATOR. His ways are not easy to understand. One thing that I did understand was that it was out of my hands...and in...the hands of OUR HEAVENLY FATHER. My prayer support group helped me feel that I was at least doing the only thing that I could count on, and that is prayer. This is the ad that I place in the paper...

ANNOUNCEMENT 1000
CATHOLIC PARENTS OF GAY CHILDREN
Prayer group forming Pray in your own home. For information write: **PRAYER GROUP** **P.O. Box 3116** **Mission Viejo, CA 92690**

When we receive inquiries, we send this reply...

Dear Fellow Parent,

My sixteen year old son "came out" to his father and me last September. Our comfortable Catholic world came crashing down around our shoulders. He is the youngest of five children, all heterosexual. No one in our family has had any contact with the homosexual world except for those people that you meet as hairdressers or store clerks etc. We have no idea how this could have happened or why? We have sought professional counseling within the faith, but no one seems to have any answers for us. Our only hope seems to be God himself. I love my son dearly. My main concern is for his soul. I know that God loves our children even more than we do. Someone needs to pray for them. We parents are the ones that God has given them to. To birth—To raise—To nurture and, I believe, to pray for. Parents, I feel, are the only ones who would be willing to pray for them faithfully every day of their lives. I personally believe that is what must be done: —Daily Prayer— It matters not which prayers a parent chooses as long as it is consistent. Daily Mass is, of course, the best if that is possible. Any Mass offered for the salvation of a soul has infinite merit. The rosary is great. Calling upon our Blessed Mother to join us and help us in our needs is a great comfort. She is a powerful friend and ally. Praying to her under Her title of "Mother of Perpetual Help" is very widespread. I believe Our Dear Lord would have a hard time saying no to His Mother. After all, we are mothers asking his Mother to help us. St. Jude is a powerful friend. He is the patron saint of Impossible and Hopeless cases. What to do about a gay child seems to fit here. I have also discovered the Novena to the Divine Mercy and Chaplet. I will enclose all of these prayers. Novena to our Lady of Perpetual Help-Novena to St. Jude. Novena to the Divine Mercy and Chaplet-Prayer to St. Michael the Archangel. If you have your own private prayers and devotions please feel free to use them instead. I feel that even a Hail Mary or an Our Father said faithfully every day is better than no prayer at all.

In our busy, hectic, work-a-day world, we don't seem to have a lot of spare time. I use my driving time to prayer advantage. I turn off the radio and talk to God instead. Also while doing the dishes, or preparing dinner or waiting in line at the Super Market, you can do a lot of praying. If it is really a hectic day, with no time at all, there is always bedtime. Brush the teeth, wash the face and say at least one Hail Mary. Tomorrow I'll do more, but never less than one prayer a day. Sometimes my husband and I hold hands and pray together. One Our Father, One Hail Mary and One made-up prayer from the heart. These times seem almost miraculous in their results. But remembering Our Lord's words, "Whenever two or more are gathered together in my name, there am I in the midst of them."

So Fathers and Mothers, any time you can pray together you are taking advantage of that promise. *So do it.* With a Novena we tend to think that nine days of prayer is going to take care of our problems. With a Gay child, I feel we will say these prayers for a lifetime of consecutive nine days — over and over. Without being "preachy," I guess we know that our whole life is spent trying to get to heaven. God is trying to help us save our souls, and our ancient adversary "the devil" is trying to drag us to hell. Our souls are a battleground. Good against Evil. What we are doing here is waging war for the souls of our children, and our only real weapon is prayer. So let's use it and raise a united voice to heaven. Dear God, please grant our children salvation.

I am in a no-man's land on this homosexual issue. I do not understand much about it. I have lots of questions. How did it happen? Why did it happen? Could I have done anything to prevent it? Did I do anything to cause it? What does God think? Why Me? I have no answers to any of these questions. I only know one thing for sure. My child did not choose this. It rather seems to be something that he "is." A condition that happened somehow to him. He has known since grammar school that he was different. He kept it a deep dark secret to himself. He was very religious. An altar boy, planning to be a priest. That has all been put aside now. He no longer goes to church. He knows that he is going to be rejected by the church if he falls in love and wants to be with someone. Since coming out he has joined a Gay support group. As his parents we try to show him all the parental love and stability that we can... Next to that we pray...

Won't you please join us and pray for your child, and mine, and all gay children. Let's raise a united voice to Our Heavenly Father. Dear God... Please show us the way. Dear Blessed Mother, please pray for us.

Sincerely,

JESSE DAVIS

P.S. Enclosed find a variety of prayers; choose any or all. Just say them every day.

A year later we sent this follow-up.

Dear Parents of Gay and Lesbian Children,

Thank you for your letters in response to the prayer support group. I hope that in prayer you have found comfort and solace. Keep up the prayers. Our kids need them. I've learned a lot in this past year since my son came out at age sixteen. I've talked to a lot of parents about our wonderful children. The story is similar-a very loved child-special-talented-loving-kind-compassionate-learning at a young age that they are somehow different. Not really understanding their feelings... Not knowing why, but keeping it to themselves. They grow up year by year: 3rd grade, 4th grade, 5th grade, 6th grade and then, around 7th grade, they start to try to come to grips with it. There isn't anyone that they can turn to. No one to confide in. No one to understand or help them cope. So they keep it a secret. All their little school chums are heterosexual (straight). They are very afraid to tell their parents for fear of being rejected, losing their love, maybe even being turned out of their homes. The secret is closely guarded until sometime in the future. Until some circumstance forces it out, or they just can't hide it anymore. It is especially to these little kids, living every day in frustration and worry, that my heart goes out to. OUR OWN CHILDREN HAVE ALL GONE THROUGH THIS. I feel that there is something to be learned from this. Everyone sees the teen or adult homosexual, but I don't think many people consider the child. —If they did— they would realize that Homosexuality is not a choice, but rather something that happens to you like the color of your eyes.

I have contacted a wonderful priest who heads the official Pastoral Ministry to the Lesbian and Gay Community. His name is Father Peter Liuzzi O'Carm.

He shared with me the official stand of the Catholic Church which clearly states that Homosexuality is not a choice, but an orientation one discovers in oneself. After hearing this I started taking it one step farther in my mind. I came to the realization that Our Heavenly Father somehow allows this to happen. **I Now Have A Lot More Questions Than I Have Answers.** I will keep you all posted as I continue searching for answers. Please keep up your prayers for our children and their Spiritual good, that God may keep them from harm, and lead them to be all that He wants them to be. Be sure to pray for these young children in grammar school, to help them cope, and to help their parents to understand them, and love them.

Sincerely,

Jesse Davis

CHAPTER THREE

WHAT DOES THE CHURCH SAY?

Next step! Contact the Church!... Find out what is going on within the context of my Faith. I called the Chancery Office in Los Angeles. They referred me to Father Peter Liuzzi. He heads the official Ministry to the Gay and Lesbian Community. He was appointed to this position by Bishop Roger Mahony. I made an appointment to see him through his secretary Marge. He is a marvelous, kindly priest and very comforting to talk to. He stated the official positions of the church.

The church is well aware of the fact that Homosexuality is NOT A CHOICE. "It is an orientation that one discovers in one's self."

I realized that this is a *very* non-committal phrase. I *think* it translates to mean: YOU ARE GAY... YOU DO NOT FEEL ATTRACTION TO THE OPPOSITE SEX... INSTEAD YOU FEEL ATTRACTION TO THE SAME SEX...

Whatever the child's age when they start to figure this out, they cannot understand how or why it happened. They do not have any idea how they are going to live their lives in an upside-down, backwards way to the rest of the population.

Father Liuzzi explained the further thoughts of the Church. "It is not a sin to be a Homosexual" BUT "It is a sin to commit a Homosexual act." There was also some mention of diminished responsibility.

There is an ongoing Ministry in the Church to welcome Homosexuals to stay within the Church, to remain in a state of grace, attend Mass, receive the sacraments, and remain celibate.

Father Liuzzi is deeply understanding and compassionate. He is very kind and willing to listen. You instantly feel how much he genuinely cares about every word you say to him. Thank God for someone who cares.

Further church teaching on the subject says that all sexual acts must be limited to the covenant of marriage... AND...

All sexual acts must be open to procreation.

This being said, how does a Homosexual go about living a real life, just like everyone else? God has given us FREE WILL. We are *all* supposed to be allowed to choose.

To marry...or to remain celibate.

To marry...or to choose a religious vocation.

A nun— or priest— *choose* to offer their celibacy, as a sacrifice to God, in the sacrament of Holy Orders. Both of these instances are *choices.* Both are acceptable to the person doing the choosing.

In the first case, to marry, or remain a celibate bachelor. If you choose to marry, you can have love and partnership and sex "legally." On the other hand, if you choose bachelorhood and remain celibate, it is a choice freely chosen because you want to. If the going gets rough, and you can't live without love and sex in your life, you can reverse your decision and get married.

In the other case of Holy orders, or Vows, the "Beloved" is God Himself, Loved above all other things or beings. A special calling from God, to live a committed life, consumed with love for Him, and forsaking all others. Dedicated to *His* service, in a life of prayer and service, and filled with grace. VERY SPECIAL INDEED. Again, it is a life freely chosen.

The homosexual, on the other hand, is not allowed to choose. He must remain celibate whether he wants to or not.

— He is not allowed to fall in love.
— He is not allowed to marry.
— He is not allowed the companionship of a lifetime partner.

— He can either remain celibate
— *or* remain celibate
— *or* remain celibate

This is where my reason forces me to ask: Why would God single out these people to be condemned to a no win-no answer-no solution situation. These people all start out the same as we do. They come into this world as human infants. This is not the way OUR HEAVENLY FATHER does things. He is all merciful and all loving. Why would He make the "Natural Law" for *all* people and then deliberately create 10% of the population to be Homosexual human infants? They are unable to function as a Heterosexual and not allowed to function as a Homosexual. They may not know at birth what they are, but very early in life they do become aware. My son tells me that he was in preschool when he became aware of his difference. There was a picture of a cute guy on his lunch pail that he had a crush on. There was also a boy who was very special to him in his Montessori School class. He became very attached to him. He cried and cried when the little boy moved away. He must have been between the age of three and four...and he knew...

JUST THINK OF IT...

In Nursery Schools, and Pre-Schools, and Day Care Centers, and homes all over the world. In other countries, and other cultures, in cities, and towns, and villages, where schools and centers don't even exist. As early as three and four years of age, 10% of children are becoming aware that there is something different about the way they feel.

Considering the fact that God created these people, how can we know why He created them this way?...

What did He have in mind?...

What is His plan?...

We do know that people cannot consciously and deliberately choose their sexual orientation, nor can they decide to change the orientation they have. We do know that a person's sexual orientation is basically established at a very early age. Even though it may take years for the person to recognize and acknowledge it.

CHAPTER FOUR

WHAT DOES THE BIBLE SAY?

God moves in mysterious ways his wonders to perform! An old saying, but true! About a year and a half before my son "came out," we were in a parent and student Preparation Encounter for the sacrament of Confirmation. I had some questions about the new guidelines for the reception of the sacraments. Some teachings I had grown up with, such as the early Baptism of infants, Original sin, and the actual existence of Adam and Eve, were being treated as if they were unimportant and not to be taken literally. Being a traditionally conservative Catholic, I was disturbed by the attitude of the priest conducting the class. I contacted the coordinator for the religious education department who was in charge of the program. I wanted to know where these new teachings were originating. I was told that this is what they were learning in the seminaries these days.

At my request, she obtained for me the actual textbooks that were being used. I started with *Who Wrote The Bible* by Richard Elliott Friedman (see Note 2). He presents an in-depth inquiry into the actual authorship of the Pentateuch, originally attributed to Moses, but subsequently found to be derived from various sources within Judah and Israel. Next I launched into *Reading the Old Testament,* an Introduction by Lawrence Boadt, C.S.P., Associate Professor of Sacred Scripture at the Washington Theological Union in Washington D.C. (see Note 3). This textbook is an instructional guide for the serious Bible student. I spent the next two years dissecting the Old Testament. Little did I realize at the time how important that study was to become, as a scholastic background in the compilation of this chapter of my book.

In 1984 I had the good fortune to be able to spend several weeks in the Holy Land on Pilgrimage with a Catholic priest and a Jewish scholar turned Catholic priest. We were a small group of twenty pilgrims, seriously devoted to a study of the important sites of the Bible in the Old and New Testament. We were able to celebrate Mass on-site in each location, and study the Bible readings that pertained to each happening. It was wonderful. It really brings it all to life...

As I am prompted to write this book, ten years later, I am grateful for my experiences. You have to go back mentally, thousands of years, and consider the life and traditions of the writers of the time... To understand the attitudes of the present generation about homosexuality, we need to delve into the past...

Let's take a look at the Bible! (See Note 4.)

Our Lord, during his lifetime, never said one word about homosexuality.

The Ten Commandments do not address homosexuality.

The only places that homosexuality are addressed in the entire Bible are:

> Leviticus 18:22 and 20:13 (*both written by the ancient tribe of Levite priests over thousands of years ago in a holiness code.*)
> Genesis 19:1-25 (Sodom and Gomorrah)
>
> *(The following are all written by St. Paul)*
>
> Romans 1:25-31
> Corinthians 6:9-10
> Timothy 1:10

Let's take the first one, Leviticus 18:22:

> "You shall not lie with a male as with a woman; such a thing is an abomination."

And the second one, Leviticus 20:13:

> "If a man lies with a male as with a woman, both of them shall be put to death for their abominable deed; they have forfeited their lives." [See Note 4]

My personal observation of these two references in the Holiness Code, put together by the priestly tribe of Levites, is that they are part of an endless list of rules and regulations put together for the Jewish people of the time. Some of the laws make sense, and some of them do not. Some of them are downright silly. Such as: *Do not put on a garment woven with two kinds of thread... Do not tattoo yourselves.* These same laws are the ones that Our Lord faced during His Public Ministry. The Pharisees used them to try to entrap Him. Jesus rebuked the Pharisees for their constant stream of laws that did not always have meaning or relevancy. This was thousands of years ago more or less. Nothing at that time was known about genetics. No one knew anything about God creating children with genuine homosexual orientation. These PARTICULAR laws seem to apply to *heterosexual* people who were immoral by *choice,* who turn against God and seek sexual pleasure for personal gratification as their only purpose. These were not moral people who merely had an unchosen same-sex orientation.

In Genesis: 19:1-25 (Sodom and Gomorrah): This is a very mysterious passage. I have read it and re-read it. I invite you to do the same. There is not *one* specific mention of Homosexuality. It is obvious that the people were wicked. The Bible states that, "The outcry against Sodom and Gomorrah is great, and their sin is very grave." The Bible does not state what that sin or sins are. There seems to be a state of thorough wickedness. The Angels (known to us as angels, known to the townspeople as men) are strangers to the people of the city. They demand to have them sent out, that they may abuse them. What abuse this is, the Bible does not clarify. Do they want to beat them? Do they want to rob them? Do they just hate strangers? Scholars more learned than myself have never been able to agree on the exact sin. The vast majority of opinion seems to feel that it is a sin against hospitality. The medieval rabbinical authority, Nachmanides, composed a commentary on Genesis 19, arguing that their sin was clearly a sin against hospitality and not anything sexual (see Note 5). He states that their intention was to stop people from coming among them, for they thought that because of the excellence of their land many would come there, and they despised charity (see Note 5).

Jewish tradition did not associate Sodom with Homosexuality, but rather with sin in general (see Note 6). The use of the term "sodomy" to refer to a specific form of homosexual activity does not originate with the Old Testament, but is a later usage. The name being used to denote homosexual activity of a licentious nature, rather than homosexual activity practiced in a true loving orientation, of monogamous nature, originates in Medieval Europe (see Note 7). Thousands of years ago, in Old Testament times, and here, I am talking about Genesis (Sodom and Gomorrah, and Leviticus) the people on the earth who worshipped THE ONE TRUE GOD were religious Jews. All others were pagans. Pagans worshipped false gods. They had all kinds of gods. Pagans believed that all misfortunes were the result of the gods being angry with them. To placate their gods they had to make sacrifices. One of the horrible types of sacrifices that they made to their gods was human sacrifice. In fact, they sacrificed children to their false gods. They also had temples built to their gods, and in these temples they kept temple prostitutes, male and female. In their worship services they committed all manner of sexual acts in the name of temple worship. They also practiced bestiality as part of their worship services (see Note 4). When the religious Jews encountered these people, they tried to stop these evil practices. No more sacrificing of humans. No more sacrificing of children. No more bestiality. No more temple sex rites. No heterosexual acts, no homosexual acts, performed as worship to stone idol gods. They had to put a stop to all of these things.

When these people went to war and conquered their enemies, they did various things to celebrate their victories. They drank the blood of their enemies. They also raped the women. And they took as much of the population as they wished as slaves. The conquering leader also killed the conquered leader of the enemy troop. But, before he killed him, he usually did some rituals to express superiority over and contempt for the victim. One of those rituals was to publicly rape him as a sign of domination and to humiliate the victim. These sexual practices of worshipping and conquering were abominations to the religious Jews who lived chaste and moral lives in obedience to OUR HEAVENLY FATHER (see Note 8).

The ancient priest of Leviticus, in laying down the laws, addressed all of these issues that were so sinful and disgusting to them. The ancient Levite priest, however, had no knowledge of true homosexual orientation, in which a person finds themselves unable to function in a heterosexual condition. It seems inconceivable that God should use true orientation homosexual love as a trial for humans if it was prohibited by Him.

Now, leaving the Old Testament behind, we look at the New Testament and St. Paul, as he seems to be the only one who mentions this subject. Romans 1:25-31 refers to pagans who adore Idols:

> They who exchange the truth of God for a lie, and worshipped and served the creature rather than the Creator who is blessed forever. For this cause God has given them up to shameful lusts; For their women have exchanged the natural use for that which is against nature, and in like manner the men also, having abandoned the natural use of the woman, have burned in their lusts one towards another, men with men doing shameless things and receiving in themselves fitting recompense of their perversity and as they have resolved against possessing the knowledge of God, God has given them up to a reprobate sense, so that they do what is not fitting, being filled with all iniquity, malice, immorality, avarice, wickedness, being full of envy, murder, contention, deceit, malignity; being whisperers, detractors, hateful to God, irreverent, proud, haughty, plotters of evil; disobedient to parents, foolish, dissolute, without affection, without fidelity, without mercy.

This is quite a condemnation it seems, on a group of idolaters who seem to be so wicked that they leave no stone unturned in their sinful natures. The fact that this particular group of heterosexual sinners, among their other transgressions, committed unnatural sexual genital acts along with their long list of sins, does not specifically apply to people born with same-sex orientation. To single out this verse to prove the case against homosexuality means pointing to one sin committed by a group of thoroughly sinful people and pointing to it as if it were the only important part of the passage. These people are accused of committing so many varied sins that it seems that they are entirely evil. The primary sin is idolatry and a refusal to accept God as their creator. The fact that it states that they have given up the natural uses of men and women in sex means that at one time they had done the opposite. They seem to be heterosexuals engaging in sinful genital activity because of their wickedness. There are twenty-three types of sins attributed to them including murder, malice and deceit. Saying homosexuality is the object of the verse is like pointing to a drop of water and calling it an ocean.

Corinthians 6:9-10 states:

> Or do you not know that the unjust will not possess the kingdom of God? Do not err; neither fornicators, nor idolaters, nor adulterers, nor the effeminate, nor sodomites, nor thieves, nor the covetous, nor drunkards, nor the evil tongued, nor the greedy will possess the kingdom of God.

Timothy 1:9-10 states:

> Knowing that the law is not made for the just but for the unjust and rebellious for the ungodly, and sinners, for criminals and the defiled, for patricides and matricides, for murderers, for immoral people, for sodomites, for kidnappers, for liars, for perjurers and what ever else is contrary to the sound doctrine.

All of these verses are by St. Paul who is attacking every sinful action that he can think of. He has been on multiple journeys and has seen Greek temple prostitutes in idolatrous sexual acts. He must have been particularly scandalized by these encounters because he refers to them in all of his lists of sin condemnations. These are extremely evil practices to the religious Jews. These passages also pertain to idolaters who worship something other than God, who refuse to worship God. In their wickedness God leaves them to pursue all sorts of sin and self-destructive behavior. Unfortunately, modern day fundamentalists use these writings pertaining mostly to Greek temple prostitutes and idolaters to condemn the 10% of the population who are born homosexual. This could not have been the original intent as nothing at that time was known of genetics or true same-sex orientation.

CHAPTER FIVE

FAMILY-MOM-DAD-SIBLINGS

Where do homosexuals come from? Could something in their lives cause them to be this way? I have heard it stated that domineering mothers produce sissy boys who eventually turn into gay boys. Or is it mothers who overprotect? Society can't seem to make up its mind. What about lesbian daughters? Doesn't that happen when Dad wants a boy and gets a girl instead? Maybe he exposes her to too much football. If these simplistic theories sound a bit silly, it's because they are. They come from people who are looking for a place to lay the blame, for something that they have no knowledge of, nor any explanation for. They only know that they disapprove. This author has interviewed countless sets of parents. Although some of them took the news of family homosexuality a little harder than others, I didn't find any of the people to be anything other than average people. None of their family histories had anything unusual about them, except for one. One of the grandmothers of a very nice young man had survived a Nazi's concentration camp during World War II. That is definitely a very unusual experience, but I do not believe that it had anything to do with her grandson turning out to be a homosexual. The estimate that 10% of the population is gay is probably a very conservative estimate.

Out of every one hundred babies born, 10% are likely to be gay. You can bet on it. They have a *straight* mother and father. They have *straight* brothers and sisters, who *marry*, have kids and live normal everyday lives. They have *straight* grandmothers and grandfathers. They also come equipped with *straight* uncles, aunts and cousins. Not to mention all of the friends and classmates throughout their school years who go through life with them every day and never have a clue.

You will find them playing with toys, playing with other kids, and going to school. They also participate in sports, belong to boy scouts-girl scouts etc. They do chores, go to church, fight with their brothers and sisters, ride bicycles, skateboard, surf, play football, baseball, and karate.

Sound familiar?... It should. It's what all kids do. You might ask?... Could something be different about the background of this particular boy?... What was *his* father like?... Let's take a look...

His father lived in the same blue-collar neighborhood throughout his grammar school and high school days. He played baseball in grammar school, got good grades, and built model air planes. He had very average blue-collar relatives. A movie was a big night out, and camping was a special vacation. He was on the gym team in high school, and went on to win an All City Championship on the side horse for Pepperdine College in Los Angeles. He maintained very good grades, took a few years off to serve time in the United States Coast Guard. He became an engine-man, and finished his stint as a first class petty officer. He continued college on the G.I. Bill. He became interested in the building business, and ultimately became a land developer. As far as his personality is concerned, he is amiable, easy going, and very much a man's man. He enjoys boating, water-skiing, snow-skiing, motor-cycle riding, camping and racquetball. He likes people and works hard. He's kind and generous and fun loving. He is loving and kind to his wife and children. He is a convert to Catholicism. Devout and practicing. I can't ask you all about your opinion of this man, but I can say that he seems pretty average to me.

Next let's take a look at mom. She was raised Catholic, attended Catholic schools, and was brought up on the Baltimore Catechism. She came from the same type blue-collar family. She grew up in the same neighborhood... She is very family oriented, and loves being a housewife and mother. Prior to marriage she had her own apartment, was a bookkeeper, and did lots of dating. After spending five years on the single scene, she was ready to settle down to marriage and a family. Married life was always very exciting to her. She was young and in love. Setting up housekeeping in a home of her own and having adorable babies and great kids made life a great ongoing adventure.

There were crosses to bear. We all get them. There were two baby girls lost in childbirth. This was very hard to adjust to. When you are looking forward to holding a baby in your arms, and you feel it moving within your very being, you begin to feel a love and feeling of protection toward your child before birth. It is a very empty, sad feeling to have them taken away from you. It is a time of grieving. But nothing prepared me for the terrible tragedy of losing my twenty-month-old son in a drowning accident. The grief was so overwhelming that I didn't think I could go on. You do somehow. One day follows another and years march on. And you just keep functioning until time allows you to come back to caring about life. It takes years. Something my parish priest said to me at that time comes to mind, pertaining to this trial twenty-six years later. I was in an agony of self-blame. If only I would have noticed that the combination lock was not properly attached. If only I had not answered the door. I went over and over a litany of self-blame. The priest kept reassuring me that it was not my fault. No matter how conscientious a parent is, accidents do happen. I was having none of it. It definitely had to be my fault. It was then that he very sternly told me that this had been Brian's last day on earth. If God had meant for him to have a further life, then he would not have died. That if he had not drowned, then it would have been something else. He would have developed rapid pneumonia, or something, and died in his sleep. Whatever the method, that was all the life that God had allotted him on this earth. But I continued, if only the lock had not been put back on improperly. Then Father said, "If God had planned that Brian's life were to continue he would have sent his angel to close that gate." I finally understood what Father was trying to say. Life and Death and our destinies are in God's hands. When God makes decisions we have to say "Thy will be done."

By the same token, even though I do not understand why some people are born homosexual, I realize that God must have something in mind or it wouldn't happen... We went on with our lives. We had three more sons. Our lifestyle revolved around the home, our children, school life, homework, camping, boating, love and laughter. Of course, we went to church on Sunday, and weekday mass as often as we could fit it in. Our boys became altar boys. Our lives were very wholesome. Morality and honesty were practiced. As I look on our lives as Catholic parents, except for the heartache of losing our children, (*which is one of the hardest things that God can send a parent*), I feel that we were pretty much like all the other Catholic parents that we knew.

Our oldest son graduated from Servite High School and then entered the family business. He is married and has three children. Our daughter went to Cornelia Connelly and then tried running an English Horse Riding School. It didn't offer a lot of profit so she turned to real estate. She met a wonderful young man and married. They intend to start a family soon. Our middle child went to Mater Dei High School. He entered the family business following a couple years of college. Two years ago he met a lovely young lady, they married, and are expecting their first child. The next youngest boy graduated *cum laude* from the University of San Diego. He is trying to decide if he would like to be a college professor or have a rock and roll band. He's a drummer with his own band. He also has a very nice girl friend.

All of this sounds pretty mainstream. I feel that we are like multitudes of everyday people. Doing ordinary things and living ordinary lives. I can't find anything in our lives that fits the textbook reasons for homosexuality to appear. Life can start to feel pretty comfortable. We were approaching what are considered "The Golden Years." We thought we were on the downhill side of life. We had been married thirty-five plus years. We had raised our children. We were grandparents. We had worked long and hard. I looked forward to our ending years, watching our children raise children, and doing our share to help by offering to baby-sit or whatever. All this *complacency* came to an end the day our youngest "came out" to us in the beginning of his junior year of high school.

He had been moving toward this day for many years. In his very young years he did not have to face it or deal with it. All he had to do with his life was go to school, do his homework, play with his friends, do his chores, obey his parents and teachers, go to church and behave himself. When he reached junior high, he did what the other kids were doing.

They start getting social, going to skate-night with their classmates, getting together with the other kids on the weekends to go to the movies or the beach. By the time he reached his freshman year in high school, the other guys were asking girls to go to the movies, or to a party, sometimes one-on-one. When it was appropriate to invite a date, he did just that. Until the beginning of his junior year, when he was sixteen and a half, everything progressed at a normal pace. It was at this point, when his romantic instincts surfaced, that he had to face the fact that he had always been a homosexual. The only romantic interests that he felt were toward his own sex. He had no interest in girls whatsoever. This is pretty typical of all the young men I have interviewed. They reach junior high and they try to date girls. They want to be normal just like everyone else — mainstream. Kids of this age try to please their peers. At least they try to fit in. They dress alike. They talk alike. They surely don't want to be different and strange. They try very hard to be like everyone else. As they go through the ritual of dating girls they find out that it just doesn't work. They can like girls as friends, but that's as far as it goes. They feel absolutely nothing romantic toward them.

As they grow older, and get farther along in high school, at least by age seventeen or eighteen years of age, they have to face their dilemma. No matter how hard they try, they can't be something that they are not. They are confused and worried. What is going to become of them? How can they tell their parents? They can't... How can they tell their brothers and sisters? They can't... They need desperately to talk to someone. They need counseling and guidance. Where can they find someone to talk to? Where can they find other people like themselves who will understand their feelings and what they are going through? I think that everyone is aware that teenagers face a lot of problems growing up.

Typical kids from good stable families have turbulent teen years, are unsure of themselves, struggle with school grades and parental understanding, and have peer pressures to experiment with sex and drugs. They have uncertainties about their abilities, and they even have concerns about their looks and degree of popularity. Nobody wants to be a geek. Just ask any parent. They can tell you how their well-adjusted, happy, sunny pre-teens, turn into cranky aloof strangers. How many parents hear the statement, "You just don't understand me!" Can you imagine how much harder this rite of passage is for a homosexual child? It is a very heavy burden.

They are different — other guys don't accept them. Not only are they rejected, they are also harassed. They try to get by. They try to survive. Believe me, they keep it a secret as long as they can.

After they come out they really start having problems. Now they get massive rejection. By their mothers and fathers, sisters, brothers, aunts, uncles, cousins, grandmothers and grandfathers, teachers, counselors, friends, schoolmates, and the public in general.

The suicide rate for homosexual teen males is very high. I'M NOT SURPRISED!...

They are social lepers. They have to worry about every person they encounter. They get a lot of negative reactions. Everything from being considered an oddity, to seeing people being repulsed or suspicious. The reactions go all the way to hatred. How would you like to have your child go through this due to no fault of their own?...

Chapter Six

Promiscuity

The next issue that needs to be addressed is promiscuity. Within the Catholic Church, the young men that I have met who are gay are well aware of God's laws concerning sex. They have studied their catechism all along. They are really confused as to what to do with their predicament. Many of them do enter the priesthood. There is no life for them under the present dictates of the Church or society. Belonging to a community of priests is a sort of family. It is certainly better than a life of solitary loneliness. Coming home from a job, to an empty house or apartment, for sixty to eighty years, is certainly a dismal prospect. What would be your goals?... Who needs a house without a family?... Why take vacations?... There's no one to go with. Everyone else gets to have someone with them. You get to go alone. I am not saying here that homosexual priests who have a genuine vocation to the priesthood have any reason to join the clergy except that of a real desire to serve Almighty God. I'm talking about the young men who join the priesthood because it is the only vocation open to them that gives any meaning or purpose to their lives. A lot of them leave the cloth when they realize what a challenging job it is to be a true man of God. A vocation is a marvelous thing. Thank God for priests. As a Catholic mother I have always had a secret wish that one of my sons would become a priest. What a joyous blessing that would be. Mothers of priests must be a very happy breed.

Those young Catholic men who cannot do justice to the job and leave the priesthood are in a no-man's land.

— These young men cannot turn to anyone. The Church has no real answers for them except "live with it." Their families and

friends are embarrassed to even admit that they are gay. Society
has no understanding or compassion for them.

— Young men who have *not* had a religious upbringing have
a whole different set of standards. They have no rules, they have
no guidelines. What are they supposed to do or think? Society
believes them to be an oddity and an abomination. Whatever
they do, they are going to hell so it doesn't matter what they do.
Gay men have *active sex drives* and without any purpose not to
become promiscuous, they do become promiscuous. Some *date,*
some pair off in relationships. Some *commit* to a lifetime relationship. I feel that their actions are equivalent to the diversity in
normal average society. In everyday society as we know it,
straight men have *active sex drives*, some become promiscuous,
some *date,* some pair off in different types of relationships, e.g.,
"Living Together." Some *commit* to a lifelong relationship of
marriage. In a responsible Christian society, young men and
women date, become engaged, and get married. If they practice
their religion, they remain celibate until they get married. They
then raise a family and live a life of mutual love and support,
raising their own families to love God and live in harmony.
Other people who have not had the benefit of a religious standard
opt to live other lifestyles that are not as ideal.

— Promiscuous people can lead pretty irresponsible lives.
Other decent people who do not live by a religious ethic prefer to
live together in an unmarried state. Some are afraid of responsibility, some are not sure enough of their feelings to commit. Yet,
they don't want to live alone. There are many other types of
families also.

Single parents raise children out of wedlock, on their own.
Divorced fathers and mothers have to raise families on their own.
Grandparents, in this modern era, are raising their grandchildren.
Friends and relatives sometimes live together as families — if
they are fortunate enough to have friends or relatives who are
available. Gay men and women who love each other and want to
commit to a lifetime relationship live together as a family.

I personally do not believe in promiscuity. I believe in remain-
ing celibate until marriage. There is a silent majority of Gay
people who are decent, upstanding people, who do not believe in
promiscuity. They live everyday lives just like everyone else.

They go to work, come home to their partner, fix dinner, watch TV, wash the dishes, take out the garbage, and get ready for work the next day, just like everyone else. You won't notice them because they are just average people, living everyday lives. They do not "cruise" looking for one night stands, or go to bath houses, or act in any other irresponsible ways. They do not belong to militant gay rights groups. In fact, they deplore these highly visible bad examples because it gives the decent gay community a bad name. The media loves this sort of news; it's sensational, gets a lot of notice, and sells a lot of newspapers. There is nothing newsworthy about gay people who live their lives quietly, go to work during the week, and have friends over to play bridge or have a barbecue on the weekend.

There are other Gay people who are more visible than their quieter counterparts. They are the guys who have more feminine attributes (hormones maybe). Their actions are more noticeable because their voices sound feminine. Their actions are more female and they kind of stand out in the crowd. I know many of them very well. Outside of their female tendencies which attract attention, they are great people. They are kindly, with a good sense of humor. They probably should have been born as girls. Something in the development process perhaps didn't work properly. There are a lot of birth defects, and guys who should have been girls, and girls who should have been boys are probably among them. These people go through life feeling like they should have been born the way that they feel. It's too bad that they didn't; then they wouldn't have any problems.

Another myth that needs to be dispelled is that homosexual men are pedophiles. This misconception causes all parents of boys to be leery and suspicious of all Gay men. Pedophiles are mentally disturbed people. They molest children of both sexes. They molest little boys and little girls. They produce child pornography. In my opinion, they are criminals and should be put in a mental institution for the criminally insane. Pedophiles occur mainly in the heterosexual community, probably because 85% to 90% of the population is heterosexual. When pedophiles are discovered in the homosexual community, it gives a wrong impression for all Gay men. It is assumed that their attraction is due to the fact that they are homosexual and not to the fact that they are pedophiles. This is a seriously damaging misconception.

Another wrong impression is that Gays will try to "recruit" or "change" straight males or females into Gays, as if you could train a person to be gay, or talk a person into being gay. This is such a ridiculous theory that if you think about it, you would realize that there wouldn't even be any Gays. They would have all been talked out of it by their parents at the very first sign. Can you imagine trying to talk a straight male out of the fact that he is attracted to girls? The attraction is there. It is a fact, and nothing can change that fact. Boys like girls, and girls like boys, unless they are homosexual. No amount of talking or cajoling can change that. Just ask any straight male you know if you could talk him out of an attraction for women. Ask him if you could "talk" him into dating guys instead of girls. And then be prepared for him to think you are insane. The facts are that gay guys are attracted to other gay guys because they have the same type of qualities that cause them to be gay in the first place. They really prefer to be in the company of their own kind as that is the place where they can receive the most understanding and be themselves without feeling out of place, and an oddity.

They tend to live in ghettos of their own making. That is why you will find large communities of Gays in Laguna Beach, West Hollywood and San Francisco. They are comfortable and welcome among their "own." They can look at a straight man and see with their eyes that he is attractive. But they know in their minds that they would be treated with repulsion and anger — *even violence* — if they so much as thought about approaching him. In fact, the minute they get to know the guy they would find his personality and whole manner of being so different from anything that they are attracted to, that they would quickly change their first thought. Gay men are attracted to other gay men. They have normal type relationships with them in a very regular matter of fact way. Again, we see everyday people living everyday lives in everyday houses across the land, minding their own business.

CHAPTER SEVEN

CHOICE OR ORIENTATION? ACCEPTANCE

I feel that now is the time to take a completely different look at Homosexuality! With modern science suspecting the causes of same-sex orientation to be genetic, it is time to dispel the myths of choice. The medical professionals that I have spoken to say that it is just a matter of time until the results are published. Over and over I have heard the same statement from Gays. "Why would anyone want to choose to be Gay on purpose?" This statement is followed by other reasons such as: "It is such a lonely life!" or "Who would choose to live outside of society and be so hated?"

IT IS NOT A CHOICE!

When people are born a certain way through no choice of their own — such as race, or looks, or handicaps — should they be penalized by society? Is that *fair?*... I think not. An innocent child of six years of age knows nothing of sex. Nothing about his orientation is based on his knowledge of sex. His puppy love "crushes" are based on the same kinds of little immature feelings that all children feel at that age. They are directed toward the same sex, but the child has no way of understanding the "WHY" of the situation. It is time to rethink this entire issue. People should be aware of their children and their differences. If you *think* your child might be gay, *get him or her into some counseling.* It is a very frightening and lonely time for kids, and they need all the help they can get. How would you like to be upside down and backwards?

There need to be counselors on school campuses. I have watched, with some dismay, the attempts at this sort of counseling being initiated by gay support groups at the High School level. This is the age that these kids have to come to grips with this situation for the first time. They are immediately misunderstood. Groups spring up right away to protest. These protests must be fueled by fear and misunderstanding. Perhaps the people doing the protesting think that these groups are formed to promote promiscuous behavior. This is not the point. Perhaps they think that this is an attempt to recruit straight kids and teach them to be gay. This is ABSOLUTELY UNTRUE! Perhaps they think that this is an attempt to promote gay rights. This is certainly not the purpose! Perhaps they think this is a way to unite Gays so that they can promote militant causes. This is not the reason!... WHAT IS THE POINT? WHAT ARE THEY TRYING TO DO?... *These support and counseling groups are actually formed to help kids who discover that they are gay, to cope with a hostile life.*

They need someone to talk to. Someone who will understand what they are going through. They need to tell their parents that they are gay. *They do not know how to do this.* The counselors can help them explain things to their parents. They can help the parents cope with this painful and stress-filled fact. They can help the kids stay in school. They can encourage them to avoid *irresponsible* behavior. A gay child is so alone in the world that they need help in just getting through every day in a normal manner. They already have problems, believe me. The other guys in school have already noticed that they are different. They are reviled and harassed.

In my son's case they threw him against lockers in the hall. They threw food at him during lunch time, along with lots of insulting verbal abuse... For a young man of sixteen, this is pretty hard to handle. My son never said a word to me about this.

How could he?... I didn't even know that he was gay. He tried going to the counselors at his school. They weren't too eager to talk to him because they did not even want to acknowledge that they had a gay kid in the school. He spent a lot of time crying. He just went out to the parking lot and sat in his car and cried. When the school authorities discovered him there, he was told to return to class and was given detention. By December he felt so out-of-place that he asked if he could change schools. We agreed, and he enrolled in the local public school. It didn't take long for the people at the new school to figure out that he was gay and it started all over again. He finally did home-study for the rest of the year. He then took an equivalency test, passed, and that was the end of High School. He was lucky, as he had parents who loved him, even though we rejected his homosexuality.

Other kids are not as fortunate. Some of them are thrown out of the house. Most are rejected by home and school. All of them have emotional problems. The suicide rate for homosexual male teens is the highest rate of all suicides. The whole world is against them. Where can they go? Perform a mental exercise and just imagine one of your very own children living through this scenario. I don't think any of us would wish this on one of *our* favorite young people. Can you imagine if every time your child walked out of the house everyone treated him, or her, as if they were unwanted and unwelcome? The looks they receive are full of derision, and the treatment they receive is unkind and demeaning. This is not what anyone would want for their child.

It is time for people to accept that these kids deserve to live a life of acceptance in society just like everyone else. They are a part of the human race, just like everyone else. They are different from the "norm," but so are people of different races and creeds different from each other. So are people who are blind, or have other handicaps, different from the "norm." So are people with Down's syndrome, and other defects, different from this "norm." Are they *all* supposed to be second class citizens? I guess you are really lucky if you are fortunate enough to be born one of the lucky ones who gets to be one of these "normal people." And may God have mercy on you if you are not... People around the world have been giving a lot of lip service to the word PEACE. They also talk about **BROTHERLY** LOVE, and wouldn't it be great if everyone practiced it. Gosh, there wouldn't be any **WARS**. It's time to practice what we preach!... At least give these people a chance to live their lives without hostility.

Gay people do live on the same planet with the rest of us, and before these people are gay adults, they are gay kids. Instead of pretending that they don't exist, let's give them some mainstream guidelines just like we give all of our other children. God created all of us equal in His eyes. We need to live under the same rules and regulations if we are supposed to be chaste before marriage. And isn't that what God *teaches,* and *all parents,* and *all of society* really want to happen?... *Unfortunately* this is not what really *does* happen!... That is obvious! All you have to do is look at the history of statistics to see that this doesn't happen the way that we want it to. But we teach our children as if we expect them to *behave* as we teach them. We don't just say, "Oh well, you are going to do wrong anyway, so why bother?" No! We don't say that to our kids! We teach them with all the sincerity, and hope in our hearts, that they will behave themselves as we want them to, and *postpone sex* until marriage. We try to enforce this by monitoring their friends, their time and anything else we can control. Then we hope and pray for the best. We need to give these same guidelines to gay kids. We need to realize and accept the fact that they are going to date and keep company with members of their same sex just like heterosexual kids do with the opposite sex. When they find the right person, they are going to commit to a lasting relationship, just like all the other young people in the world. This is the way it should be. It's what all people of average background and standard behavior do. They should not be abandoned to a moral garbage dump of — **You Are Gay** — so it doesn't matter what you people do. You are going to hell. So just be promiscuous anyway and hide under a rock. Because no one wants to know that you are here anyway. If we handled all of our children in the same manner that we treat our gay children, I would hate to see what a sorry mess our world would be.

Let's do something realistic about these kids. Let's discover them at an earlier age when we can help them cope with their differences. Let us get counseling for them so that they can embark on living a regular life just like everyone else. Next face the fact that they do not Choose to be Gay, nor can they do anything to change the fact. Then let's help them live their lives in a responsible way just like everyone else. Let's teach ALL of our children that promiscuous behavior results in all manner of unwanted consequences, from unwanted teenage pregnancies, to a variety of venereal diseases including AIDS. The realities of immoral and irresponsible behavior are devastatingly tragic. Also to be taken into consideration are: loss of innocence, loss of self-respect, and a loss of moral values. This is certainly enough reason for any parent to give their child all of the guidance and proper upbringing, that they are humanly capable of.

CHAPTER EIGHT

GAY OR NOT GAY?
HOW CAN YOU TELL?

How can you tell if your child, or brother, or sister, or cousin, or friend is gay? I can only say that we didn't see it. It was there all along and I just did not connect the signs. As I look back on it, I can be more truthful with myself and admit that I didn't want to see the signs that our son was gay. When his brothers teased him and called him a little fag, I punished them for picking on him. When I spotted two of his classmates in a toy store, Brent was looking at the girl toys. I overheard them say, "Should we say hi to him, or should we just leave the little faggot alone?" I thought that they were very mean ill-behaved children. After all, it wasn't his fault that he was a sissy boy. He was a nice kid. I thought that he would outgrow it by the time that he reached High School. Our son was a bit more emotional than the other boys in the family. He cried easily. He had a very high-pitched voice as a small child. This left him, thank heaven, as he left adolescence and he sounds like a guy now. When he was younger it sounded very whinny. He played with girl toys — dolls, dishes, hopscotch, jump rope — and he preferred to play with the girls. He was very artsy. He excelled in creative writing. He's a great dancer; it's in his bones. He has a lot of acting ability, dramatic and flamboyant. He was always kind and gentle and very aware of other people's feelings. He was afraid of the dark. He didn't fight. He didn't swear. He didn't spit. He doesn't like cruelty or wars. He is very aware of his looks, and if he has a bad hair day, it's a real catastrophe. He likes the theater, the ballet, soft music and reads endlessly. He also played on a soccer team and took a karate class when he was in about the third grade. He did physically tear into his siblings when necessary, and likes to ride dune buggies in the desert.

Other gay guys that I have interviewed also showed some of these traits. They were definitely more "sissy." They are nonviolent. They are creative. They cry. They are gentle. They also like to do some of the things that straight guys do, like sports and playing video games. Another thing that played a big role in his life was his imagination. There were imaginary friends and games. Our back yard was an entire kingdom. He will be writing an entire series of fantasy fiction books all created from his childhood.

This may or may not help, but if your son seems softer and less aggressive than the other guys, it might help to check it out.

If I had known sooner, I definitely would have started counseling early enough to do some good. I feel that we could have helped him get through school, and hopefully on to college. He wouldn't have had to go through all of the emotional trauma and anger that he felt toward us, and the rest of the world, because no one understood him and he couldn't turn to anyone. He hopefully could have gone on with his life in an orderly fashion. As it is, without a college education, a career is going to be hard to come by. He will have to return to some kind of study. He has spent the last two years coming to gripes with life as a gay. It takes a long time for them to settle into this. They have to come out to all of their friends and see if they will still be their friends. They have to see if their friend's parents will still accept them. They need to approach all of their relatives individually and check the situation out, so it's trauma over and over again.

Gay people in the music industry have written some songs about this problem. One of them sadly asks the question of his mother, "Do you still love your little boy?" They don't know the answer to this question and they have to find out. For all of the parents who have questions such as, "What did we do wrong? Were we too hard on the kid, or too soft? Should we have done some things to toughen him up, like force him into sports?", when you go through counseling, you can have these questions answered. There is an author out there who thinks that if you do "Reparative Therapy" that you can turn a homosexual into a heterosexual. When you exhaust all of these avenues and come to the bottom line, your child will still be a homosexual but you will have put all of the negative things to rest. You will also know that you have done everything that you can possibly do. And you do not have to be plagued with doubts. Life will take on a more positive feeling for you.

And, of course, they are going to start dating. They are going to see a cute gay guy and they are going to ask him out. They are going to go through all of the same kinds of situations that straight guys go through. They are going to get turned down. They are going to get their feeling hurt. They are going to get accepted. They are going out on that date, and are going to think that this person likes them, only to be *dumped* next week. All of these things happen to straight people and, believe me, they happen in the same way to Gays. My son did some dating, experienced a lot of emotional trauma, and did some more dating. He has settled into a permanent relationship at last and is very happy. His boyfriend is very nice and comes from a very nice family. This is just as important to a family relationship in a gay relationship as it is for all families. You will want your gay son or daughter to settle down with someone nice. And you hope that they come from a nice family. All of the gay children that I have interviewed have had very nice families. Except for the fact that they have a gay son or daughter, they are like all average nice people. I haven't met any mean people or any weirdoes.

If you can discover the gay child in your family soon enough, I think you can help them a lot in facing all of these "Rites of Passage." Hopefully you can help them cope with the negative things that are going to happen to them in the form of rejection. They are going to be rejected. They are going to be reviled by some. They are even going to be hated. Unfortunately, there are even some people out there who will want to physically hurt them just because they are gay. Black people can really relate to this as they have had to suffer this cruel injustice since the beginning of time. Just because of the color of their skin. Thank God that this racial prejudice is subsiding. I personally did not participate in racial prejudice because, thankfully, my parents treated all people equally and had friends in all races. I did not know that racial prejudice existed until I reached high school and witnessed it being practiced by my peers. I was appalled and very sad. I always spoke out against it and befriended all who were the victims of it. I, myself, did experience some prejudice, growing up Catholic in the 1930's. When a playmate was forbidden to play with me because I was Catholic. It was very puzzling. Things like that are hard for a child to figure out. You are being treated as if you have done something wrong, and yet, you don't know what that "something" is. Little did I know that sometime in the future my child would go through this because he is gay. As parents you can't prevent it, but you can be there for them with love, understanding and support when it happens.

The important thing here is still, OUR KIDS. Let's try to keep them in school longer. Let's help them go on to college. Their whole career depends on this. I am not sure of what the best way to accomplish this is going to be. A counselor can certainly help here. Not "coming out" so soon might help. At least not until after high school. It may not be the best answer, but getting through high school is a very important hurdle. It is a wonderful accomplishment in itself and can do much for your child's self-esteem and sense of accomplishment... "Dropping Out" is negative, and no matter how necessary they feel that it is at the time, it has to leave them with a sense of failing to do something that they really needed to do. They can always take *time out* after graduation to come to grips with, and *"Find"* themselves before they go off to college. Even if they don't go to college for a year or two, they can still do it.

When you find out that your child is gay, it is a good idea to join a support group like PFLAG (Parents and Friends of Lesbians and Gays). This group is for families, and makes things a lot easier, especially in the beginning. If you can get the siblings and extended family to go as well, it would make family life a lot less traumatic. For Catholics there is a group called Koinonia. Their main office is in Orange County, California. Then please, pray for them all of their lives. They are going to need your prayers every day.

CHAPTER NINE

REJECTION

This is one of the saddest and hardest aspects in the life of a homosexual child. When you are born into a family, you are a part of it. You are welcome. When you come home from school in the afternoon, you are accepted as a member of the household. Even if you fight with your brothers and sisters, you are still a member of the group. If you are disobedient and need to be punished by your parents, you know that when it all blows over things will be back to normal. And that you will be "OK" with the clan. When a homosexual child "comes out" this all changes. He is now an oddity. He is no longer "OK." He is not just one of the kids anymore. He is decidedly different. He is no longer a member of the group. They are the "in crowd," and he will be forever on the outside looking in. They are not really welcome anymore. They now are tolerated to a degree. When they come into a room, they are no longer greeted with acceptance. They are looked at with a coolness that chills to the bone. Eyes that once looked at them with openness are now guarded and veiled. Brothers and sisters take a step back as you approach them, and they talk to you as if you were a visitor to the home instead of being a part of it. Did I say visitor? In actuality it is more like an intruder, a stranger. These people who used to be your flesh and blood now talk about you. They whisper about you behind their hands. Conversation ceases when you walk into the room. You are no longer invited to join in on family activities. This can include something as simple as going to a movie as a group. Or something as hurtful as being left out of a birthday party or a Mother's Day Brunch. You are not included anymore, because they don't want you anymore. This may not be the case with all homosexuals, but according to the individuals I have interviewed, this is an all too common occurrence.

Pretend that one of your very own straight children were singled out, for some unknown reason, for this type of treatment. Would this situation not break your heart? Would you not want to do something for this poor kid, to make his world turn back to normal again? Rejection is extremely hurtful and lonely. Some religions practice a form of this with people who have fallen from their perception of grace. I believe they call it shunning. I have read about it, and it seems that the victims of this treatment find it devastating to deal with.

There is more to it than this. It actually gets worse. By the very nature of the situation, the problems become more and more complex. Brothers revile you. They want no part of you. They cannot understand where you are coming from. How can you not like girls? How can you possibly be attracted to other males? Why are you different? Whatever the answer, they want no part of it. A girl could kiss your lips and it would be OK, but if another male was to give you even so much as a peck on the lips, it could almost make them want to throw up. You hear words like GROSS, YUCK, CREEPY. It's as if you had suddenly contracted leprosy or something.

Mothers of sons in the family suddenly do not so much as want you to be in the same room with their boys. They have known you and trusted you for a considerable length of time, maybe years, MAYBE YOUR ENTIRE LIFE. All of a sudden you are no longer to be trusted. I do not know if they fear that you are going to molest their sons, or recruit their sons, or teach them deviant behavior. Maybe a combination of all three. But you are going to suffer the embarrassment of being suspected of some sort of wrongdoing that you have no intention of committing, even if you knew what it was. In the first place, you are not a pedophile. And never have been, and cannot even imagine why anyone would think this to begin with. Everyone in the family has known you since birth. How can you be different today from who you were yesterday? You were not suspected of being a pedophile yesterday. How could you have changed into someone else in one day?

As far as recruiting others, to be as yourself. How can this be accomplished? A person has to have an orientation inborn. You can't turn another person into being a homosexual by discussing the subject. You are having a hard time getting your family to accept you. Why would you complicate this by behaving in an irresponsible manner? You don't want to do anything to turn them against you. Things are bad enough already. This is your family. They are looking at your every move through a magnifying glass. Why would you do anything deliberately to make your situation any worse than it is? You would have to either be crazy or a sadomasochist. Remember we are not talking here about a real pedophile, or a mentally sick person, or a criminal, or a bad sinful person. We are talking here about a decent law-abiding youngster who wouldn't harm a fly. We are talking about a family member who has never given anyone any trouble. A kid who has never done anything more sinister than fight with his siblings, sasses a little bit, and get an occasional D on his report card. That was yesterday; today he is public enemy number one.

Brothers, sisters, cousins, etc., are not the only ones who behave in this unkind and un-Christ-like manner. Mothers and fathers also behave in less than a parental manner. There are fathers who have physically abused their sons, as if they could beat it out of them. Even if they are not that extreme, they do reject their sons and let them know what a disappointment they are to them. They let them know that, as far as they are concerned, they will never be OK. Mothers for the most part are usually not as severe as fathers; however they do initially reject the entire situation. They are angry. They are hurt. They are bewildered. They cry. They cannot believe it. They feel that it is their fault. They feel like they are a failure. Some of them come to their senses after the initial shock and realize that this is their child and that they still love him, no matter what. Some of them can never forgive their sons for not being what they want them to be. Other mothers fall somewhere in between. Some take a year or two to heal. Some get over it quickly. Some never get over it.

Your author took about a month and a half to be able to treat her son with any real normalcy. It was about a year before things really calmed down. I finally realized that I loved my son no matter what, and that is all that really mattered in our relationship. And yes, I was still his mother, and he still was my "little boy." I was much happier when I arrived at that point. Brent's father handled it better than I did. He wasn't as emotional as I was about it. Even though he must have been unhappy about the situation, he was kindly and decent about it. He tried to understand and help. God bless him, he is a good man. How did the rest of our family take it? WELL...

Our oldest son believes, as the church does, that Brent should remain a celibate bachelor for his entire life. His wife, my daughter-in-law, feels uncomfortable about having my grandchildren around their uncle. He loves them dearly, and this hurts his feelings. He deals with it on a day to day basis. She and Brent had been close before he "came out." They were buddies. She thought of him as her little brother, and was very sweet and loving to him. Her distancing herself from him really broke his heart. The hurt is still close to the surface, and recently, in an emotional moment, he accused her of abandoning him. I feel that time will heal this, and they will be close again as she is a very loving and good-hearted person. Our daughter and her husband accepted it better than the rest of the family; however she does lecture him excessively about AIDS. They do love him, and that is what really counts. His next older brother, the middle child in the family and the most mellow, is politely distant. He keeps his distance and goes about his life, not being involved any more than he has to. Brent always idolized this brother, and followed him around like a little puppy dog. So this one hurt a lot. His wife, who has only known Brent for about two years, has been kindly and accepting. They get along well. The next brother is six years older than Brent. They were never really close. Their relationship has had a lot of ups and downs. Sometimes there are long periods of peace between them, and at other times there is a lot of tension. In recent times there has been a trend toward goodwill.

Here you have a mixed bag of reactions, most of them emotionally difficult for a teenager to deal with. Brent has hardened his heart and tried to live his life in a partial denial. He goes on with his daily living without making an issue of the rejection. When he is faced with it, emotions come to the surface. He becomes angry and he cries, and the next day he tries to get on with his life and not focus on yesterday. So far it has been working for him, but I know he would be so happy if they all just loved him as if he were their brother. It hurts him to see their

friends being treated like brothers and himself being treated like
an outsider.

Other gays I have interviewed have not fared as well. One
woman spoke to me of her twin brothers. They were fraternal,
not identical, twins. One of the boys was gay. His brother hated
him for their entire lives. She remembered the straight brother
constantly delivering physical abuse to the gay brother. She said
that he used to throw him to the ground over and over again. The
gay brother, who was a professional dancer, contracted AIDS
from an unfaithful partner in the early days before much was
known about the disease. The hostile brother then developed
some remorse, and plans on treating his brother with some kindness before his death.

Another mother of five sons, one of whom was gay, had
another story to tell. Her husband is a blue-collar factory worker,
and was into lots of "guy type" activities such as fishing and
hunting. He relished taking his little troop off into the wild on
hunting trips. They were also, *big time,* into sports. All of the
boys were involved in various teams: baseball, football, soccer,
etc. The gay child showed no telltale signs of orientation, and did
not come out of the closet until he was in his twenties. His parents and brothers were in such complete shock that they immediately disowned him. He was banished from the group. His
brothers would have nothing to do with him. Eight long years
went by, with this unfortunate boy being shunned by his family
and living in loneliness. His mother was miserable. She is
Catholic and spent most of her time making novenas, offering
mass and praying through her tears. One day she woke up and
came to the realization that *she* was depriving herself of the
company of her son. The only person standing between herself
and her son was herself. She was depriving herself of a relationship that she sadly wanted and needed. She loved her son; she
missed him. She picked up the phone and called him. Needless to
say, he was more than happy to welcome his mom and reconcile
with her. She and he were very happy to be back to normal
again. She now visits him and his lifelong partner in their apartment, enjoying a long lost mother-son love. She confided to me
that she is happy again and at peace. She regrets eight wasted
years. She still prays for her son, and trusts in God's mercy.

A few weeks ago I read in a national newspaper that a man noticed a sissy boy tendency in his two year old son and beat him to death because he thought that he might turn out to be a homosexual. This tragic incident points up the horrible extremes that homophobia can take. This author could not sleep after reading this article. I pray that all people who read this book will treat homosexuals with tolerance and kindness. I hope that their families will treat them with understanding and love. I think that every family member should stop for a minute and realize that it could have been themselves. *That they could have been the one to have been born with a gene for homosexual orientation instead of the sibling who was born that way.* And if they mentally put themselves in that person's shoes, perhaps they would have an entirely different perspective. I think that would bring about a lot more understanding. It would certainly save a lot of heartache. With the homophobia that exists today, coupled with intolerance from society, and rejection by both society and family, it is no wonder that the suicide rate for adolescent gay males is the highest in the world. Please let's change that. Start with yourself, and reach out to others. The life you help may be closer to you than you think!

CHAPTER TEN

LIFESTYLE

The homosexual that no one notices is the plain, ordinary person next door who has no intention of drawing any notice to himself. He is the silent majority of the gay community. He is a policeman on the neighborhood force going about his job just like the other guys. Nobody knows he's gay. His fellow officers would be very surprised. I saw a true-story television program recently about coming out. The police officer on the show was duty officer in his precinct and no one had the slightest knowledge of his orientation. He decided to march in the Gay Pride Festival in his city. When his fellow officers, guarding the parade, saw him, they couldn't believe their eyes. They were flabbergasted. (After the parade, some of his fellow officers treated him differently.) These people are the firemen, the teachers, the doctors and the nurses. You will find them in your exercise class. You will find them in the pew next to you in church.

Some sound like Gays. They have a sound to their voices that is recognizable as gay. Some do not sound like Gays at all. Some act more feminine. Some do not act that way at all. You would never guess in a million years they are gay. I have met a couple of gay guys who like to dress up like girls on special occasions like Halloween. One of them would love to wear high fashion women's clothes on a model's ramp. He probably has a few too many female hormones. He is really a nice young man, with a very nice personality. He is no threat to anyone. He just would love to model high fashion women's clothes. I know another young man who loves to cross dress. He is funny and has a very happy, positive attitude. He has done some acting in movies, and is always "on." The world is his stage. He is a lot of fun to be around and finds it great fun to dress up like a girl and fool people. He makes a better looking girl than he does a guy. He also probably has too many female hormones, but he is harmless. There is a hairdresser that I have known for many years. He is Italian, and comes from a very nice Catholic family. He has three very straight brothers. Two are married and one is still on the prowl. He has not dated anyone for eight years because he wants to get his life and career on track. He told me that with the threat of AIDS that he is in no hurry. I bet that his lifestyle does not fit the mental image that most people have of gays.

The truth of the matter is that there are millions of gays "out there," living quiet, conservative lives, responsible, productive lives, creative lives. They are law abiding, tax paying citizens, just like anyone else. Their only difference is that they are attracted to a life partner of the same sex instead of the opposite sex. The more noticeable Gays are the ones with perhaps a few more female hormones for the guys, and a few more male hormones for the girls. The guys have feminine characteristics and female sounding voices. These are the hairdressers (there's that creative ability again), sales clerks, etc. that we see every day. Some of the girls are very athletic and have a high profile in active sports. A lot of the girls don't have any unusual characteristics at all. You would never know that they were gay unless they told you so. These are the good people of both sexes for whom I am trying to gain some acceptance and understanding. They never cause anyone any trouble, and they do not deserve to be treated as second class citizens. They certainly should never be treated as an inferior by anyone.

We have all seen the ugliness of that mentality. I feel that all the good people of the earth are sick to death of bigotry and cruelty shown to our fellow human beings in the forms of racial prejudice. Superior human being over inferior human being. Ethnic cleansing, and all of the other forms of disgusting mental rot, that man can sink to in a self-imposed position of sinful pride. Tradition tells us that the downfall of the angel Lucifer, to become the Satan of Hell, was caused by his sin of Pride. We certainly have all witnessed this form of depravity in the person of Adolph Hitler. What a sickening monster he was, with his visions of a "Master Race." Thank God that there were many people, in many countries, to rise up and strike him down. When I hear of the Neo-Nazi movement today, I realize that Satan is still on the prowl. I hope that there are still enough sane people around the globe to prevent any significant return of that horror. Unfortunately, the hateful ideas that these people have, are directed toward gays as evidenced by the sorry spectacle of gay bashing. They also do racial and religious bashing. Hopefully, some day God willing, these attitudes will vanish, and we can live together as brothers in harmony. A lot of Christian people have been praying for that intention for a long time.

Unfortunately, in the gay community there are some irresponsible people who bring unwelcome notice to themselves. These people have no morals or guidelines at all. They frequent gay bath houses and sex clubs, and do all the stereotypical immoral things that people associate with all gays. They have multiple partners and seek sex only for self-gratification. They use their partners of the moment as if they were an appliance. Their behavior is irresponsible and unwanted in regular society. These are the people who cause all the trouble for the typical well-behaved gays. Parents are correct to keep their children far away from them for fear of molestation. They have given society reason to avoid them and look with distaste upon their actions. The gay community also looks with distaste at their actions.

This having been said, I would like to see ways to *change this situation.*

Why are these Gays this way?... Has anyone ever given them any reason to be any other way?... What has society done for them? WE TURN OUR BACKS ON THEM WHEN THEY REACH PUBERTY!... We literally throw them out in the street. What do parents do for them? THEY REJECT THEM... Worst of all, what do the churches do for them? THEY CONDEMN THEM TO HELL!... Is it any wonder that they are out of control?

Do you think that if they had been given any love and guidance by their families perhaps they might have wanted to behave in a more moral manner? Do you think that if they had been treated by society as if they were persons with worth and dignity that perhaps they would have wanted to live up to those expectations? Do you think that if the churches would have done their duty from the beginning, and treated these people with fairness, and given them some avenue of reality to pursue under God's love and laws, that perhaps they might have tried to live with a common moral code?

Somehow I feel that all God's people should have the same *laws,* the same *treatment* and the same *love.* Didn't our Blessed Lord come to save us all? Why do some of us have some rules, and others have no rules that apply to them at all? Should I tell my straight children, "You should be moral people and respect chastity and try your best with God's grace to remain a virgin until marriage." And should we tell our gay children, "We are very sorry, but it doesn't matter what you do. Because we have no provisions for you to live a moral life, I guess it really doesn't *matter* what you do. You don't have a chance. You're not like everybody else. You're different. TOO BAD. SORRY. Go hide in a closet and try not to cause us too much embarrassment."

There has to be another scenario here. Gay children should be counseled right along with their straight brothers and sisters that they are all loved by the same God, and that they all were given the same set of *Ten Commandments.* It is necessary for all of them to be chaste; before *marriage* for straights, or *commitment* for gays. I think that the prophets of old stood on the street corners and called all God's people to *Repent* of their sins and to return to moral ways. I think that all of the *churches* today should be standing on all the street corners of the world, calling their gay flock back into the fold. Exhort them to *repent,* and return to their God. Give them a way back to salvation. Come up with a solution for them whereby they can live a *Real* life with a lifelong partner. What are you waiting for?... If *you* don't evangelize them and call them back, what hope do they have? If they can't turn to God, to whom can they go?...*You have been negligent for too long!* It is time for the churches of the world to shoulder their responsibility and shepherd these people back to God. Where have you been all these centuries when they needed you?... I think you have been busy, being uncaring and pompous about it, with your head in the sand. I think that you are personally responsible for all those lost souls!... *Who* will *cry* for them? It's never too late to turn things around. All you have to do is get *busy* and do your *duty!*

P.S. This doesn't mean that you should get busy condemning them to their face and on street corners and in sterile little letters to the editors of newspapers. It means to look at homosexuals through the eyes of CHRIST with love, caring, understanding and, most of all, compassion. "Whatsoever you do to the least of these you do unto me."

CHAPTER ELEVEN

CHALLENGE TO CHURCH: NEW LOOK

This book is also being written as a plea to my church, the Roman Catholic Church, to take a new look at this impossible situation. The *modus operandi* of my church is to do nothing in a rash manner. They can take hundreds of years just to think about something. Once they make up their mind, they can take another hundred years just to do something about it. Sometimes they just decide to let it be, because they don't want to be the generation to change it. I know that this is an ancient situation.

As I have pointed out in previous chapters, there are guidelines that pertain to this question. The official stance of the church has been governed by a few words in Genesis, a few words in the Leviticus holiness code, and a few words from St. Paul. All of the instances in the Old Testament have been questioned by scholars more learned than myself. I have borrowed their findings and have listed them in the Bibliography. They have covered this question extensively and shed much light. All the findings are ambiguous at best. There is no hard and fast law coming from OUR HEAVENLY FATHER. And, there is no hard and fast law coming from OUR BLESSED SAVIOR JESUS CHRIST.

The only words governing an entire untold millions of souls of homosexuals is found in an ancient set of writings by Levite priests written thousands of years ago. These same documents, which were supposed to have been attributed to Moses, have been found by Biblical Scholars to have not been written by him at all. They find that they do not know who put quill to parchment. There is some speculation that it might have been the prophet Jeremiah. These books are not even attributed to one source. They were written by the tribes of Israel and the tribes of

Judah, and were gathered and transcribed by an unknown source later than they were written. There are many meanings and much speculation as to the meaning of these ancient passages. If you think anyone can know for sure what some of these ancient things actually were supposed to mean, I challenge them to explain the passage about angels finding the daughters of men to be fair. And supposedly having sex with them. This joining was purported to produce a race of giants... This mysterious passage is in Genesis. I do not think that any Bible Scholar can give an explanation for it, and so no one ever mentions it.

I do know for sure that MY HEAVENLY FATHER created my son, and that He allowed him to somehow be Gay through no choice of his own. He created all other homosexual people also through no choice of their own. I am talking here of people who have a true homosexual orientation that they do not ask for, but find that they are stuck with just the same. I am not talking at all about people who are promiscuous and sinful and who perform homosexual acts for sexual gratification. There is a big difference in these two separate groups! One group *chooses,* the other does *not.*

I do not think that anyone on this earth can possibly know what God has in mind pertaining to this situation. No one has ever asked HIM, and neither has HE ever mentioned it to anyone. JESUS never mentioned this situation. Even St. Paul seems to be talking about idolaters who were using homosexual acts as worship services to idols. This passage indicates that these people were heterosexual people, committing homosexual ritual acts.

This takes us to the Natural Law, which is supposed to be the ultimate answer. This states that every act of sexual union must be within the sacrament of marriage, and must be open to procreation. If this fact were strictly interpreted, and enforced, then no act of rhythm would be permitted. No married couple would be permitted to have sex during a woman's menstrual cycle, and it would not be permitted for couples to have sex post-menopause. We all know that this is not enforced in this narrow interpretation. Under the same guidelines how can this same law be applied to a situation that no one knows anything about.
—For Sure—

I am asking my Church here, *and I am speaking specifically to the governing body* that makes the decisions. I assume that these things are decided in *Rome* and then are passed on to the rest of us. I am asking you to once more take a look at this situation realistically and study it with the intention to give these children who grow up in limbo some hope for a normal life. Please don't double talk here. And please don't sweep this question under the carpet.

I have read a lot of so-called "answers" on this subject. They strike me as being non-answers. *(a) It is permitted to be a homosexual.* This is ridiculous in itself, as why would you need to have permission to be what God has created you to be. How could you be anything other than what you have been created to be? Does a black man need permission to be black? Does a bird need permission to grow feathers? The second part of this answer is really perplexing. *(b) It is not permissible for a homosexual to engage in homosexual acts.* Then what is a homosexual permitted to do if he cannot do, what is for him, the only thing that feels natural for him to do according to the nature that God has created him with? Then we come to the part where they answer this. He is to do nothing about his life or his situation. It is suggested that frequent attendance at mass and frequent reception of the sacraments will help him accept his cruel fate.

Now don't get me wrong. I love the mass and I love the sacraments. They are the lifelines of our souls. As a Catholic wife and mother, they are my soul's link to God and my road map to salvation. But no one is asking me to be a celibate nonentity.

I do not think here that the *issue* is important as a *sexual* issue. It is an issue of being *allowed* to *love*. What is important is having the love of a lifelong partner. A soul mate that you can grow old with, and walk down life's path with, and share with, and face adversity with, and share laughter, and joy, and sorrow with. *Sex* is a *small* part of any *human relationship* when compared to the rest of the *reality* that is *living* a *life*.

Why can't a gay couple commit to a life time of fidelity to one another, forsaking all others?...

Is it more desirable to condemn them to Hell? To send them from childhood into a no-man's land. No rules. No guidelines.

No hope. Just sweep them under the carpet and condemn them. As a church we give them no choices. As a society, we turn our backs on them. Is this what God wants us to do? I don't think so.

I understand that there is a new book on the market that deals with this situation. It is written by Yale University history professor, John Boswell. Its title is *Same-Sex Unions in Pre-Modern Europe* (Villard Books). It asserts that from the 8th to the 18th centuries the Catholic Church sanctioned same-sex unions and offered ceremonies complete with prayers for the couple's union. I had heard of this situation before. It was referred to as a same-sex commitment ceremony. I was going to try to research it myself, but happily someone has beat me to it.

This is the extent of my challenge, and my humble questioning. *Please Holy Father, Please Roman curia, Please,* look at this situation and *Please,* do something about it. Don't just let it lay in Limbo for another 1,000 years? Ten percent of the population is waiting for some kind of a reprieve from no-man's land. As a Catholic mother, my child's soul is at stake!... And I can't wait a thousand years. Jesus died on the cross for the sake of my son's soul and for the sake of all the souls of all of the homosexuals of all time. Won't you at least look at the situation and really put some people to study it this time? With the intention of getting to the bottom of the old theories from the Old Testament and look at them realistically?

Give these people a chance to join the rest of the human race. They are not monsters. They are not deviants. They are not evil. They are born as children, come into the world innocently, not knowing that they have the handicap of a God-given orientation that is going to mark them as social and ecclesiastical outcasts when they reach adolescence. *Please* give them a chance. *It is up to you.*

CHAPTER TWELVE

GENESIS REVISITED

There have been a rash of articles by religious authors in Catholic and other periodicals referring to Genesis as a condemnation of Homosexuality. This deals with the natural law, specifically Chapter 1 verses 26-28. God said:

> Let us make mankind in our image and likeness; and let them have dominion over the fish of the sea, the birds of the air, the cattle, over all the wild animals and every creature that crawls on the earth.

> God created man in his image. In the image of God he created him. Male and female he created them.

> Then God blessed them and said to them, "Be fruitful and multiply; fill the earth and subdue it."

Bible scholars attribute this writing to the priestly tribe ("P"); it was written after Chapter 2.

In Chapter 2 verse 4 there is a second rendition of the story of the heavens and the earth at their creation.

> When the Lord God made the earth and the heavens, there was not yet any field shrub on the earth nor had the plants of the field sprung up, for the Lord God had sent no rain on the earth and there was no man to till the soil; but a mist rose from the earth and watered all the surface of the ground. Then the Lord God formed man out of the dust of the ground and breathed into his nostrils the breath of life, and man became a living being. The Lord God planted a garden in Eden to the east, and he put there the man he had formed.

Verse 18 of the same chapter goes on to say:

> Then the Lord God said, "It is not good that the man is alone; I will make him a helper like himself."

And verses 21-24:

> The Lord God cast the man into a deep sleep and, while he slept, took one of his ribs and closed up its place with flesh. And the rib which the Lord God took from the man, he made into a woman, and brought her to him. Then the man said, "She now is bone of my bone, and flesh of my flesh; She shall be called woman, for from man she has been taken." For this reason a man leaves his father and mother, and clings to his wife, and the two become one flesh.

Bible scholars attribute this writing to the Yahwist source ("J") which was actually written before the priestly source ("P").

I include the entire readings because I dislike things being taken out of context. If everyone wishes to take out their Bible and check this for accuracy, they are welcome to do so. I might mention that this Bible is the *Confraternity of Christian Doctrine Edition* published in 1961; therefore it doesn't have a lot of modern footnotes and explanations and new wordings like a lot of modern Bible translations have. It's just an old fashioned, original words, Bible.

This is a beautiful passage and it appears to depict the creation of man and woman plus the explanation of the propagation of the species according to God's plan. It does not however go into the reasons that God had for creating true orientation homosexuals. And, create them He did. When an innocent child knows from his earliest remembrances of reasoning that he or she is different from other children by virtue of the fact that they are attracted to their same sex instead of the opposite sex like everyone else is, there can be no denying that God created them this way.

They have no understanding at this young age of four or five or six as to why they are different or what the implications of this difference are to be. But they are created by God as they are. This author certainly does not know what God has in mind. Nor do I know of any other human being who does either. I notice that the authors of modern day articles are calling this fact a phenomenon. A phenomenon is something for which there doesn't seem to be any explanation. Therefore how can anyone purport to know the mind of our Creator on this issue. The plan that God had in mind for man and woman in the sacrament of marriage for the co-creation of the species is obvious. The fact that this plan is obvious does not of itself give an explanation of a different reality which is that God created some people to be homosexuals through no choice of their own. This issue is undefined. I do not feel that it is in any way fair for the church to absolutely condemn an issue that is so ambiguous. At this juncture I wish to point out the second brick wall I have run into since I have been reasoning this issue. Returning to the Bible, I would like to point to this same area of Genesis to illustrate a passage that has captured my attention. Chapter 2 verse 18:

> Then the Lord God said, "It is not good that the man is alone; I will make him a helper like himself."

This is the first thing that God had to say about the situation. God, Our Father, is ever the merciful parent. He eloquently makes the profound statement that it is not good for man to be alone. He is speaking for all men, not just an elite portion. Men of the priesthood cannot be included in this example as they are gifted with a vocation that transcends the condition of mere mortal men. They are slightly less than the angels. The graces gifted to them with their vocation lead them to the celibate life, freely chosen, with God as the Beloved.

The writers of the Catholic periodicals of the day all arrive at the same conclusion for homosexuals. They are to remain celibate. In their learned opinion it is mandated that they must remain alone. It is not good for the rest of the human race to be alone. But it is good for homosexuals to be alone! How can they be so positive in their statements when their opinion seems to run contrary to the words of Our Heavenly Father?

I suggest that this is not a closed issue. It needs more study. It also needs understanding and compassion. We are dealing with human beings who just want to have the same rights that everyone else has, to love and commit for life.

So, Religious writers, please stop sounding so pompous and holier than thou. In the future, instead of being so quick to condemn, please be quick to do some research on the subject... Oh, and add a little human kindness while you're at it.

CHAPTER THIRTEEN

CONCLUSION

My first feelings were of confusion and anger. I was angry with God for doing this to me. How could He? I have always lived by the book. I was always OK. Now suddenly I wasn't OK. My kid was spiritually defective, and I took it very personally. Did God say, "Let us make the natural Law and then deliberately create people who are unable to function this way, and then condemn them?" I don't think so.

It seems that battle lines are drawn. Fundamentalists are in an iron-clad mind set which states that Homosexuality is a chosen so-called "lifestyle." The term *lifestyle* takes on a sinister connotation when used in this context. It sounds like some kind of Babylonian Orgy. I always thought that it had something to do with the style in which you lived your life such as rich or poor; country or city; party animal or stay at home. I have never heard Marriage or Holy Orders referred to as a lifestyle.

I wonder what the fundamentalists will think when they find out that it is a condition that an infant is born with. How can a tiny newborn baby be an evil abomination because he is born with a homosexual orientation that he doesn't even know that he has. Many individuals in the medical profession have assured me that the studies being conducted on the origins of homosexuality denote genetic sources. They tell me that genetics and heredity are the factors. It takes time to conduct the studies, establish the proof, and write the medical journals. But it is coming! And the medical profession has been aware of it for some time.

A study by Dr. J. Michael Bailey of Northwestern University in Evanston, Illinois and Richard C. Pillard of Boston University and their colleagues appeared in the *Archives of General Psychiatry*. This links Heredity, and The Totality of DNA Effects, with Heredity as a potent factor in setting sexual orientation.

A new study published in the *Proceedings of the National Academy of Sciences* by University of California, Los Angeles, Medical School researchers Laura Allen and Roger Gorski concerns a nerve bundle called the "anterior commissure." It is larger in gay men than in straight men. Research is continuing.

This study follows a report by Simon Le Vay, a neuroscientist at the Salk Institute for Biological Studies at La Jolla, which says that, "A brain structure called the interstitial nucleus of the anterior hypothalamus, is smaller in gay men than straight men."

Another study is being conducted at Columbia University.

Stanford University neurologist, Russell Fernald, is conducting a fascinating study on the connection between molecular events and sexual behavioral changes.

Hopefully these finding can reach a speedy conclusion that gay people are born this way and deserve to have the same rights as the rest of the citizens of the United States as guaranteed by our Constitution.

I see statements in print frequently that go something like this: *Homosexuality is a threat to Family Values.*

This is something that I do not understand at all. How can traditional marriages between men and women in any way be affected by homosexual individuals? The fact that two homosexual people decide to share a life together in monogamous fidelity seems a decent decision. How can the two couples have any bearing on each other? How can either one affect the other in any way? It seems that they are independent entities, each living a life independent of the other. How can the homosexual pair cause any negative factor to the other couple? I have heard it stated that the gay *lifestyle* is a threat to family values.

"Family Values," it seems, has become a politically correct buzzword. If a gay lifestyle is meant to connote sexual licentiousness, then it would be a threat to *any* soul: single or married, heterosexual or homosexual. But gay is not a synonym for sexual sin. It is an unchosen condition that a person is created with, that only God knows any reason why. As far as family values are concerned... A homosexual child is born into a regular family with a mother and father and sisters and brothers. He or she has been a member of a valid family since the moment of their conception. They have lived in a family and have been a part of a family all of their natural lives. In fact, they are loaded with family values! Family values are the only values that they know. How can they be a threat to what they themselves are, a member of a family with family values?

To illustrate my points, I include nine true-life stories of people who have lived through, to varying degrees, all of the issues mentioned here. I have interviewed many others and will write another book in the future featuring all of them. For now, these young people's lives are typical of a lot of their homosexual brothers and sisters. In Brent's story you get to see what I have had to say, but through his eyes. He and his boyfriend try to explain the overwhelming feeling that occurs when they finally tell someone after a lifetime of secrecy. I wrote it verbatim, and let the hesitancy speak for itself. All of the stories touch on the difficulties faced in family relationships caused by the discovery of homosexuality. Anxiety seems to be a frequently underlying factor. The participants all realized at a very young age that they were different from the other children. They all faced their hardest ordeal in telling their parents. The desire to lead a decent responsible life is evident in every story. Some of them had easier times than others. Some like Seth may never get over the traumas of their childhood. The religions touching their lives are certainly diverse: Seventh Day Adventist, Jehovah's Witnesses, Baptist, Jewish, Catholic and some unnamed. They all share an attitude that does not allow a Homosexual to function within a same-sex union. And none of them have an answer except celibacy. I hope you enjoy the stories. Please share with them their anxiety, their pain and their hope for a brighter future of acceptance and understanding. But, enough from me. In the following pages I invite you to meet the kids: Brent, Chris, Weasel, Alex, Seth, Allen, Davi, R. Jay, and Jocelyn Marie.

REAL LIFE STORIES:
CASE HISTORIES

Chapter Fourteen

Brent Speaks For Himself

The Author and Brent are mother and son. In some places Brent refers to the author in the third person and sometimes in the second person. I hope this is not too confusing for the reader. It is a little different to be writing about oneself as envisioned by another. All that praise is embarrassing but, being objective, he said it, and it's his story.

Author: How old were you when you first realized that you were different?

Brent: I was in kindergarten, and I think even earlier. Maybe as far back as pre-school. It wasn't about being different exactly. I played mainly with Strawberry Shortcake dolls and He-Man figurines when I was younger. I was more into the fantasy oriented toys. The Strawberry Shortcake dolls *"were"* actually my little friends. I would play with the He-Man figurines. I would have battles with them, but the Strawberry Shortcake dolls were my actual friends. They were people I could talk to and play with because I didn't have any real friends around home to play with. I think, looking back, it's not really that I didn't have very many friends. It's that really I couldn't relate to very many people. In kindergarten I had one friend, who was a boy. All the others happened to be girls.

In Montessori there was this guy on my lunch box; I thought he was very handsome. When I finally labeled myself, I was in fifth grade. *I was gay.* I started having sexual fantasies and stuff like that about guys. There was always a guy involved. In answer to the question, "Did I know what homosexual meant?" My brothers had always made fun of me. They called me "gay" and people in school always made fun of me. In first grade my brother Mike came over when I was getting dressed for school

one morning and called me a fairy and a fruit, and told me to
stop playing with Strawberry Shortcake dolls and stuff.

I felt very uncomfortable, not with the aspect of being a
homosexual, but that the idea of messing around sexually was
bad. I remember when I was nine years old that a friend and I
experimented by touching each other and we got caught. I
always thought after that I was wrong, but I never thought about
being gay. I always thought I was going to grow up and marry
the daughter of my mother's best friend. We were friends so we
used to say we were going to grow up and be married. The only
problem I had was my brothers or schoolmates who would tease
me and make fun of me and call me fag, and ask me if I was
queer or not. At that time I didn't have a handle on it. All I knew
was, being gay was something that you got ridiculed for. When
they called me gay or made any reference to my being a gay
person I would always say no, I'm not. Most of my friends were
girls. I felt more comfortable hanging around with them. I
wanted them to feel that they could trust me and talk to me,
because I wasn't like the other guys. I knew that I was not like
them because I was a lot more sensitive than they were. However
I never felt "in" with the girls because they still saw me as just
another boy. So they wouldn't tell me their secrets. Only two of
the girls became my best friends at that time. They shared everything with me. They didn't consider me like the rest of the boys.

Author: How did you handle the boy-girl dating issue?

Brent: I sometimes had a crush on a girl just because I liked her
and I thought she would be neat to have as a girlfriend. I never
once thought of a girl sexually. I always thought that was the
way the other boys felt about the girls. I thought that they were
strange because they did think of girls sexually. They were just
being nasty people because they thought of things like that. I
never even thought of girls like that. I was always attracted to,
and thought of doing things with, other guys.

By seventh grade things were changing. My whole entire life
had just become very academic. I became buried in study. Also I
wanted to have more of a religious edge to myself. I started
adapting religion into my life completely, and becoming a very
religious person. I would talk to people about religion, I would
hide behind a facade of being a religious person.

Author: How did the other kids treat you at school?

Brent: It varied. For the most part I felt very isolated and I felt like no one liked me. My teachers really liked me a lot.

Author: What age were you when you first came out?

Brent: I first came out at age sixteen. Before that I hadn't told anyone. I met someone at a private party and we went to dinner. I never told him that I was gay and he never told me. I tried talking to my mom about it because I had held it inside of me for quite some time. I wanted to tell her because she was my closest confidante. I talked to her one night and she told me that she could practically handle anything except for any one of her sons being gay. She could handle me being a murderer or a rapist. Or if I got someone pregnant that would pale in comparison to being gay. So automatically, that nixed that. I'm not going to tell *her* anything about me being gay.

So instead, on a Fourth of July boat party, I went to a friend of my brothers named Terry. I kept telling her that I had a deep dark secret. It was something that I had been holding inside of myself. I said, "Please don't hate me. Promise that you won't hate me. Promise that you are not going to turn away from me." She said, "Yes, Brent, just tell me." I didn't come out directly and say I'm gay. I had to keep coaxing her, to get me to tell her.

So eventually she just said, "You are gay!"...and I said, "Yes," very softly, and all of a sudden I felt very empty... I didn't understand — or feel — or know — exactly what had happened to me. I just felt empty...like... "Oh my goodness." ...I got quiet and I didn't know what to do. I sat up there, up on top of the boat. for about an hour while we went through the harbor — and was silent the whole time. I remember when I told her, and she said, "You are gay." It was like...yeah... I just felt like something went out of me. It just felt weird.

Chris (Brent's Boyfriend): It's a weird feeling... How can you describe a feeling like that emptiness?

Brent: There is no way.

Chris: That is the most amazing feeling, when you finally tell someone. Because this is a secret that you hold in your heart. After 16 or 17 years of holding this...

Brent: It feels like forever...

Chris: It's just bursting inside of you...bursting inside of you...
It's the main thing inside of you. You're thinking, how am I
going to let people know? Or how do I hide it? And all of a
sudden you just say it — and then it's out.

Brent: ...And then someone knows, and you don't know what to
do.

Chris: ...And your head is blank, and you don't feel like you
have... It's just the weirdest feeling...

Brent: It's in here, it's a feeling in here...

Chris: It's in my head. It's in my heart... It's just so... It's too
difficult to describe... I don't think unless someone has gone
through something like this that they can understand it.

Brent: Later that summer, Karen, my brother Steven's girlfriend
at the time, she and I went to a psychological self-help group.
She knew I was gay, but she didn't let on that she knew. So we
went and it was a very trying experience. I "came out" in front of
twenty-seven different strangers, which is extremely scary
because you don't know if these people, who you have spent a
whole week with, are going to reject you, hate you, or what they
are going to feel of you in general. How are they going to relate
to you? Are they going to talk to you? One of the ladies said that
she had never met a gay person in her life before. After getting to
know me, she had no problem with me being gay.

Author: That was a very strange evening for me. I had known
you all your life and I felt like I knew you backwards and
forwards. I was really close to you. Everything had been normal.
Then somehow you were different. All of a sudden you were
hostile. It was frightening. We came as a mom and dad to see our
son graduate from a personality help program, a seven day thing.
We knew it was important to you for us to be there. I didn't
know that a big deal was happening.

Brent: It was the fact that I had come out in a closed environment to a certain group of people. There were only twenty-seven
people there. All of a sudden they knew that secret about myself,
and they were safe. You and dad were not safe, because you
didn't know.

Author: You were right. I would have been entirely hostile to the whole thing. I knew something was the matter but I didn't know what it was. You were so strange and so different. You were so angry, and all that I could think was, "What is the matter with this kid?"

Brent: As for what happened after this incident, I went back to school and ran into a friend of mine who introduced me to his friends, Bonnie and May. I told Bonnie that I was gay, and she introduced me to a guy named Murphy who was also gay. He was not the best looking guy in the world, but he was the first guy that I could be set up with. We went to Carl's Jr. [a fast-food restaurant] and we made eyes at each other, and he was nice to me. Saturday of that week I went over to his house in a group. He and I started talking, and later on after everyone had left, he and I cuddled and kissed.

I thought everything was fine until the next day when my friend Sara took me out to lunch and we had a long talk. Then she told me that Murphy was HIV positive. At the time I was totally ignorant about the transmission of AIDS. In my opinion I already had it. I thought because I had touched him and I had kissed him that I had the HIV virus and I was going to die. From the look on her face and the way people were staring at me, I can only imagine how I looked. Later on she told me that I turned white as a sheet and started trembling uncontrollably. I just went into hysterics. She quickly went and paid the bill. She rushed me out of there into the car, where I broke out into uncontrollable crying. She then informed me about the ways to contract the disease and that I could not have it at all. She said that there's no possible way that I could get it from kissing.

To better understand my relationship with Murphy, you have to understand my friends, who were very peculiar people. They latched on to me and wanted me to turn against everything and everybody I had known before — like my parents and friends. They were very rude, very sarcastic. The relationship with Murphy was unusual because it seemed to encompass these other individuals.

I asked my mom if I could see Dr. Harvey because I was having some problems at school. I had to talk about the HIV issue and how I was going to relate to Murphy. Dr. Harvey

didn't even know I was gay and he had been seeing me since
fifth grade. I do not understand how he could not know I was
gay. He kept telling me, "Brent you have to macho up. You need
to go into basketball. You need to try out for more guy things."
He wanted to talk about me being gay. I had spent the entire last
summer coming to grips with this. I was gay. I had already
established that. I wanted to move on. I wanted to say, "I'm
dating this guy who is HIV, what should I do?" He comes back
to me with, "Brent hold on, how do you know that you are gay?"
Brent: It was you, Mom. You tried to get him to convince me
that I am not gay.

One night we had a Baking Club get-together at home. Mom
seemed real upset. I thought that mom and dad had an argument.
I went back to console her, and she told me that she knew all
about me and my sick boyfriend. Then she started telling me
about how I had destroyed her life. How she would not know
another day's happiness. She said I was the worst thing that
could ever happen to her. She immediately informed me that I
could not date my boyfriend anymore. I told them I wouldn't
date him. But I was going to continue to see Murphy regardless
of what they said.

One day I left a book home that I needed at school. I called
my mom and she and her secretary Ethel brought it to school for
me. Mom waited in the car while Ethel brought the book. Lo and
behold, Murphy came walking by. Ethel said, "Isn't that
Murphy?" I said, "Oh yeah, that's him." I knew he was looking
for me because he glanced at me. Right afterward mom and
Ethel followed him to his work, and waited for me at the movie
to see if I would show up. So they caught me red-handed. Here I
come trotting on down to see my boyfriend, *which of course* I
did every single day. Mom called dad, and dad came up to me
and said, "Is this Murphy?" I said, "Oh no, this is Calvin." Dad
said, "Well you better get your butt home, you're supposed to be
studying. What are you doing here?" I saw mom and Ethel out in
the parking lot, and I went and had a huge argument with them.

She took me to see Msgr. Harris, the Principal of my High
School, as a last ditch effort. He knew of a counselor that we
could go to. They were going to take me to an Irish monastery.
They also thought a hooker might change me back. The coun-

selor tried to explain to mom that it wasn't her fault. She also tried to give me a little more stability in my life. I needed stability in my life, but she was trying to give me the kind of stability that applies to an average kid, with a normal routine, who did not have all of these problems. It took the counselor a year to turn my mother around. During that year I swear that we fought and we fought, like cats and dogs. Cats and dogs didn't have such bitter hatred as I did toward my mother. Oh, I hated you so much.

Author: How were you getting along with the other members of the family?

Brent: Right after I broke up with Murphy I was trying to deal with the rest of my family. I always got along well with most of my brothers and sister. My sister Noelle and I have had our disputes. But through thick and thin we have always stuck by each other. We always love each other. Presently we are doing just fine. Her husband, Barry, came into the picture right about the time I came out of the closet. He treated me just fine. I don't think Barry has ever had a problem with me. I think he has been a very open-minded person. My aunts and uncles and I have always gotten along famously. I've loved all of them and they have always loved me. My cousin Walter and I have always been close friends before I came out of the closet. He's getting used to the fact now. He's starting to realize that I'm the same as I always was and I'm just a normal person. My oldest brother Mike and I actually got closer.

Author: I think that after you came out of the closet he felt sorry for you. They were picking on you. His brotherly instinct kicked in, and he wanted to be protective toward you. There is not that animosity any more.

Brent: I think my next older brother, Frank, and I had a little bit of a problem for a while. I think he got very uncomfortable with the fact, which is understandable. However, we never had that big of a falling out. I think he's OK with it now. Frank's a strange cat. He doesn't like anyone telling him anything about anything, what-so-ever. He has his own ideas how life is. He doesn't want anyone telling him about their point of view. In his mind it's...admirable; you have your point. Don't tell me about it. Just live your point of view, and I'll live my point of view, and life will just be hunky dory. Loulie, his wife, and I have gotten along famously no matter what; she has a cool head. With Steven things got much worse after he found out I was gay. We had always had a rivalry because I was the baby of the family. Before I came out of the closet I was talking to him about sexuality and he had said to me, "I will always stick by you because you are my little brother and I love you." We had started getting closer together then. But right after I came out of the closet he betrays me and turns his back on me. Steven always considered himself an open-minded person, intelligent and liberal. Where was his open-mindedness and liberal intelligence now?

Author: What about your father?

Brent: When I first came out of the closet, he was afraid for my life because of the HIV issue. I knew he was uncomfortable about me being gay. I also know that he accepted it, and that he just wanted to make me happy. He wanted to fix me at first, but once the counselor held the first couple of sessions and he knew that I was going to be gay, he was just going to "batten down the hatches" and here we go. Let's just ride this storm as best we can. Now he's fine. Out of all the people, I thought he would have the most amount of problem with it, and that mom would have the least. He got over it quicker than she did. He was for me, and more concerned for me, than for himself. He was saying, "Whatever you want Brent" and, "Whatever is going to make you happy." He was concerned for my well-being. My mom and dad are actually stronger than they were before. With all of the experiences that they have had in their lives, and then all of a sudden, their youngest child comes along and throws them a wallop.

Author: God and I have had a few conversation about that. I thought I was on my golden years of no more problems, just nice quiet years of grandchildren and stuff, and *bingo...*

Brent: And they say you can't teach an old dog new tricks.

Author: Are you having problems with anyone else in the family?

  Brent: Yes, my sister-in-law Lynn. Not so much with the fact that I'm gay, however; the fear is stemming from her children.

She doesn't want them to be exposed to homosexuality for the fact that they will not know what it is. She does not want them to go to school and say anything that will cause them to have problems. I don't think she's thinking I'm going to do something to them. She thinks I'm going to do something in front of them. Also she does not want them to be gay themselves. Which is crazy because you can't teach a person to be something that they are not. For example, I've been around heterosexuals my entire life. I've seen them do their heterosexual thing all of my life. It's like saying, "If you see their actions you are going to be heterosexual." Did I become heterosexual? No, because I'm gay. If you are a straight person, you can be around gay people all your life and it doesn't influence you. I know this girl who has two gay fathers and she's straight, as straight can be.

Lynn and I can still talk, but it's not like anything before. We have a lot of distance between us like a big wall that I would like to break down. She and I were very close friends when she first came into the family and I was younger. I went head over heels over her. I thought she was one of the best people in the whole world. We were really close. Then we sort of had a falling out when I came out of the closet. I was upset because Lynn was the closest person in the world to me. She started changing. I noticed it. It took a big toll on me. I don't think that Lynn ever realizes what losing her friendship meant to me. One night we had a huge, family argument, myself and my siblings. I think that was really a big eye-opener, because I really laid into Lynn and told her how upset I was. I felt betrayed by her because she turned her back on me. We are getting a little close again lately. We can joke. But there is still a tension that I can feel.

My siblings think that because I'm gay that I'm just going to slide on by. This is a good opportunity to say to them that I have a lot of worth, and I'm not going to try to slide on by. They don't know my life and they don't know my accomplishments. They don't know my goals. They don't know what I want to do. Just like with homosexuality, they have a lot of misconceptions about me and what I want for my life, and what I want for my future. They never want to talk to me about that. They never even want to concern themselves with what I really want to do with myself, and with what I have done. Maybe they will come around eventually, slowly, but surely. But it's hard when I've gotten so much abuse from them. I've gotten a lot of problems from them. That's because I was different. Because they don't understand, they try to put me down.

Author: Did you have any problems in High School?

Brent: When I hit my sophomore year, I finally started accepting the fact that I was gay. For a long time I thought it was just a faze. But eventually it began to dawn on me that it wasn't a faze. So I grew out of the faze excuse and began to accept it. Then junior year came along. That's when I came out of the closet. It's really difficult in high school because you have so much ridicule. I remember a couple of times I was beaten up. People used to call me fag when they were beating me up. People would make comments to me all the time, like when I was passing them in the hallway. They would say, "Oh, there's that faggot," and I wasn't even out of the closet yet. But people were stereotyping me. Then I remember my last day of school. I was leaving the lunch shelter. These people were throwing food at me, saying, "Get out of here, f_____ faggot." It's just a very hard, difficult thing to be Gay in high school. Because you get a lot of ridicule. I wasn't out of the closet. They could just tell that I was different.

Author's Comment: He did not act gay in any way. He did not display any actions, nor show any interest in the same sex. He just wasn't a rough guy who swore, spit, and made rude comments about girls like the other guys. He was neat and clean and gentle. He had a sunny disposition and an innocence about him.

Brent: It was a very difficult time, very trying. I didn't know where I was going or what to do. I had so many forces that I felt were against me. When I finally did come out of the closet, I didn't come out and say, "Here I am, and I'm gay," and shove it down peoples' throats. I was somewhat secretive about it. I told a select few. Of course, when one person knows, it goes around the whole school. I changed to a different school. Actually there I was accepted a lot more, because I really didn't know anybody. Also it was a public school rather than private, so people in my opinion were less judgmental. Which is quite ironic. Parochial school is supposed to be based on Christian principles. They try to be loving and kind to their fellow man, but in actuality they are more judgmental and self-righteous. It was a very lonely time period, a very scary time period. I went to The Center for Gays and Lesbians. I started the dating experience and I went through the party faze because I had to get a lot of the frustrations and energy out of myself. That's where I met a couple of very good friends. I started learning about my life and myself. My brothers accused me of dropping out of school, but in actuality it was a very necessary part of my life. I've heard later that many gay people will drop out of school. I think that during that time it's very necessary for adolescent homosexuals when they come out, to get away and search themselves. As they always say, "If you can't help yourself, then you can't do anything."

Author: Are you in a permanent type relationship?

Brent: Yes! It is the most wonderful thing in my whole entire life. I went through a trying time just before I met Chris. I dated someone who was a very co-dependent person. I learned a lot of bad habits from this person, about relationships. However, I did grow and learn what I did not want to become. I knew that was not what I wanted to be, and after I broke up with him I met Chris immediately. I met him at Denny's. [A fast-food restaurant.] I made eye contact with him. He was talking to a waitress friend of mine. When he went to use the phone, I walked up to her and she said, "Yes, yes, and no. Yes, I know him, yes, he's gay, and no, he's not taken." I wrote him a note saying my name is Brent and I'm interested in getting to know you. I wasn't even supposed to be there that night; it was a complete fluke. I just think we were meant to be. I left and came back later that night. I waited for him till about 3:00 in the morning. Just as I was leaving he pulled up in his car. He was dressed in hospital scrubs, which I thought were sort of strange, as I had never seen anyone dressed up in scrubs before. Later that week he came to a party of mine. Everyone spent the night, including Chris, but nothing happened. It was Valentine's night.

I wanted this to last because I liked him and I thought he was very nice and gentle. I liked his eyes. I thought they were very beautiful. The next night we went on our first date. We went to the movies. Later that night we were talking, and he said, "Why don't you come over and sit next to me?" So I sat next to him and we cuddled. We held each other all night long. We didn't kiss or anything like that. Then the next night we kissed for the first time. Since then I've really grown a lot. I'm no longer the self-conscious little boy that I was.

Author: Would you like to have children some day?

Brent: Yes, I would like to have children, perhaps two. I will not start planning on that until my late thirties.

Author: What about your Spiritual Life?

Brent: I do not consider myself promiscuous. I do consider myself religious. I pray to God daily, and every night before I go to bed. I try to look at the facts of what Jesus said.

Author: How are you coping with life in a straight society?

Brent: There is a lot of discrimination in Orange County, depending on the area. There are feelings of animosity that I get. Sometimes I'm fearful that people will know that I am gay and will ridicule me. I have been walking into a restaurant not even saying a word, and someone will yell "Fag" at me. If you met me and didn't know in advance that I was gay, I've been told by my family, my friends, and by strangers that they would not have a clue that I was gay. I'm not a flaming queen. I'm not effeminate. I'm just soft-spoken. I'm just an average regular person. What you do in your bedroom is your own business. I think the problem is ignorance.

Any person who is an American and can ridicule any person for anything is a hypocrite. This country was founded for the sole purpose to flee persecution. It is for every single one of us, all the children of this world. We are all created equal, every single person. I would like to support the Gay groups and the Gay communities out there. As I said before, they are important and they are integral. When people first come out of the closet they do not know what to do. They do not know where to go. If you are having problems with your life, these people are beacons of light and hope, for these young people.

Chris and I are getting married. Chris's family has been absolutely wonderful to me. At first there were some uncomfortable feelings because his grandmother didn't know. We didn't know how she was going to react because she was from the old country. They didn't want me around his little sister Merry. They didn't know what type of person I was. His grandmother found out on her own because I kept coming to all of the family functions with Chris. She asked, "Is Chris gay?" She said, "That's fine, I like Brent a lot. He's a mensch." (That's a "fine guy" in Yiddish.) "I like him better than any granddaughter-in-law." His whole family accepts me. His mom and I get along famously. Adam, his step-father, and I get along really well. When I first met Sal, Chris's step-mother, I was uncomfortable. The first time we went to visit we had a lot of guidelines set on us. We couldn't sleep in the same room. That has all changed. So I had some animosity in the beginning. She had her feelings and I had mine. However, she is a very dear woman. I value her friendship and her love. I think she is one of the best people that this world has to offer.

His father and I get along very well. He is a wonderful man, again one of the finest this world has to offer. I love his little sister. His whole family and I get along wonderfully. Chris's other sister Linda, is coming around to seeing me as a person and not a homosexual and we get along very well.

I want to say thank you to Chris for helping me through the ending stages of adolescence. He is the love of my life and I would give my own life for him. There is no one else in this world that I would like to share my life with. Except, of course, for my mom. My mom is the second one. My mom is someone entirely separate from the rest of the world. This is my opinion. You have two people who are very special. Your spouse who is the most important person in your whole entire life. However removed completely from the whole universe is your mom, who can never be replaced. It's not that she's the most important person in my life, or the least important person in my life. To me, she is just mom. There is no measurement you can place on a mom, saying she's the most wonderful person in the world. She's just mom... She's a pillar of strength. She's someone you go to when you need her. She's someone you have wonderful times with. And someone that you love and you cherish. I mean, I cherish my mom.

Author: Boy, all that praise. I feel like you're talking about someone else.

CHAPTER FIFTEEN

CHRISTOPHER'S STORY

Author: What age were you, or what grade in school were you, when you first realized that there was something different about your feelings?

Chris: In the second grade I felt uncomfortable about it, because I thought about guys. I didn't know if other boys felt the same way or not. Somehow I knew I was different, but I didn't know what it was. I knew I was not interested in girls. I felt weird about that. I thought it was because of my sister or my mom. They brought me up and I didn't particularly have a father image. I always remember looking at boys instead of girls.

Author: Who was the very first person that you ever shared the knowledge with?

Chris: My friend Craig. We were on a ski vacation. I told him while we were in the Jacuzzi.

Author: How old were you?

Chris: I was seventeen, he was sixteen.

Author: Did he have a clue before you told him?

Chris: No. He had no clue. However, he thought it was weird that I never had a girlfriend and never talked about girls.

Author: Did your mother have any inkling?

Chris: No. My mom had no clue.

Author: How old were you when you "came out" to your mom?

Chris: I was seventeen and a half.

Author: How did she take it?

Chris: I was sitting at the table, and I asked her, "What would you say if I told you that I was gay?"

I was kind of joking around with her at the time. She said, "I wouldn't do anything. I would still love you because you are my son." Then I said, "Well, I am gay." It took me three times to say that, *"I am gay,"* before it sank into her that I wasn't joking, and she knew that I was serious. I don't remember a lot about our conversation, other than a cold wall being constructed in a matter of ten seconds. She seemed to handle it quite well but what I didn't know was that for about three weeks she would secretly go to her room and cry. She was afraid to let the family know and she was depressed because she was never going to have grandchildren or a daughter-in-law from me. It took her about nine months until she totally accepted it. I would like to mention the fact that I was very close to my mom. We were like best friends. I wonder if gay males are closer to their mothers than straight males. Little did she know how much joy she would receive by gaining another son-in-law instead. Now she is totally accepting about it. She loves Brent and respects our relationship. In fact, she is going to be participating in our wedding.

Author: Was she married to your step-father at the time?

Chris: Yes.

Author: How did he take it?

Chris: He was shy about it. I think he was a little uncomfortable about it like most people would be. However he was comforting by stating, "Whatever makes you happy." He was a Lieutenant Colonel in the Air Force and I was in the military too. I feel at the time he was uneasy about it, but it didn't get in the way of our relationship.

Author: What about your grandmother?

Chris: That was just recently; I was 20 years old when I told her. She kind of figured it out because, for the past year, Brent and I were always together. We always came over together. So she asked my mom. My mom said, "Yes, Chris is gay." She accepted it pretty well because she liked Brent and knew that he came from a nice family.

My grandmother and step-grandfather both like Brent. They called him a "mensch," which is Yiddish or Polish for "a number one guy."

Author: I love what Chris's mother had to say about Brent. She said, "I'm so glad that Chris has Brent, because no girl would be good enough for him."

Chris: (To Brent) You were there when we told my grandmother. She was kind of fun about it. She didn't have any problems. I think it was from being in the concentration camps in Germany during World War II, imprisoned with homosexuals. She knew from personal experience that they were very nice people.

Author: What about the other side of the family, when you told your father?

Chris: I didn't tell them. It kind of went around the grapevine. It went from my mom, to my sister, from my sister, to Sal my stepmother, from Sal to my father — like a little chain.

Author: How long ago was this?

Chris: About two and a half years ago. I was eighteen.

Author: Did he call you?

Chris: My dad is kind of like me. He didn't show much emotion; however Sal and Linda made up for it. Sal called me. She is the talker of the family. Sal and Linda were crying. I was uncomfortable around them for about a year. They all belong to the Baptist Church and, as most people know, they preach against homosexuality. They felt it was just a phase. When they said that, I thought, "How can it just be a phase when I've been like this, and felt like this, for my entire life?" They thought I was confused. Linda said, "It's because we have a dysfunctional family." At the time they didn't understand and didn't seem to want to accept it. It was a trying time for us. We've worked through it. I feel we have gotten even closer. Sal and my dad are also going to participate in our wedding. They treat Brent like he is part of the family. My sister Linda and her husband Jim also have accepted me more and have fun with Brent and I.

Author: Tell me about your relationship with your stepmother.

Chris: I was about three years old when she became my stepmother. She treated me like her own child. She used to tuck me in and read bedtime stories to me and scratch my back. We are close. We went to the beach together. We traveled together. I stayed with them in Florida during the summertime. They took me to Australia. I was treated like a child of the family.

Author: How about your sister, Linda. Were you close?

Chris: We were very close. I was her little brother. She took care of me a lot. My mom was single and had to work, so my sister had to take care of me for most of the day.

Author: When you were in high school did you have any problems with the guys. Did any of them give you a bad time?

Chris: Not one problem. It was in my senior year that I really came out. It really came out because I was around Belinda. Everyone in school knew she was gay. First, all of my group knew about me, and then it got out to the rest of the school. People still treated me the same, which is actually amazing. The people at my school were very open. I went to the prom with a guy and two girls.

The guy was gay, we kind of just went together as a group. It wasn't a problem in High School. I had no problems with teachers. In fact, I gained more friends in my senior year even though they knew that I was gay.

Author: Did anyone ever break your heart and make you feel really bad? Did anyone really hurt you?

Chris: Yes. I've had the same situations in relationships as most people have had family wise. I was really hurt when Sal said, "I feel like I have lost you." At that point I did feel lost because she is my other mother and I love her. I was so frustrated because I felt that I was the same person I was before. However I felt that a burden had been lifted from me because I had finally revealed a secret which had plagued our relationship for quite some time and had finally been released. It was my dad who said to Sal, "That it's OK, he's still Chris."

Author's Comment: That actually comes from a feeling of pain, and it's a statement born of pain. Say you didn't want your son to become a priest, and he decides to be a priest anyway. You might feel like you have lost him. You get perfect thoughts in your mind about your children. You get expectations about your children. You think that they are going to be a certain way.

Chris: An incident happened with my little sister that I have always remembered. One day Merry and I were sitting in the car waiting for Sal and my dad to come out of a hotel room. Merry started asking me questions about girlfriends. At the time I had a boyfriend but, of course, I had to say it was a girlfriend. Just seconds after I quit talking, she turned and asked if I had a boyfriend... I was shocked!... She was nine years old and grew up in a hick town down in Florida. I never expected a comment like that out of her. At the time I had to answer "no," because my family didn't know. She was the first one of all my family to ask me if I was Gay.

It seems like my family from the Old Country, like my Uncle Joe, took it a lot easier than my American family.

Author: Did any of your friends treat you any differently? Did it affect any of your friendships?

Chris: There were a couple of friends who kind of went away, but now they are back.

Author: What about in the service? Did you have any problems in the service?

Chris: Oh yeah! When I first went in, before Clinton, for Basic Training I didn't have a problem. But when I went out for my Combat Medic and Practical Nurse Training I would hear jokes about Clinton's Army and gay people in the army. I just got tired of that sort of thing, and I decided to get out.

Author: Did anyone suspect that you were gay?

Chris: No one suspected me. However at the end I let a few of my friends know. There was a girl private from Alabama who was never exposed to homosexuality and she was very prejudiced against it. During my last couple of days out there I told her why I was going home, that I was gay. And she said, "Well, you really turned my head around. Because I never thought of gay people being like you."

Author: So, is there anything that you can think of that is unusual, Chris, that you would like to share with people who are not gay? Something that would help them to be more tolerant?

Chris: The person that comes out of the closet and tells people that he is gay is the same person that he was before. It doesn't change a person. Prejudice is the fear of the unknown. Prejudice is being afraid of something. What a person does in their own bedroom is their own business. I work in a hospital. I don't bring my sexuality to work. I do my job. It's not the place to have any sexuality in the public eye, for a man or a woman, in the work place. I'm going to be just what society says, quote-unquote, "I am just like a normal heterosexual person, Christopher Shire."

The trouble is that the media focus is on homosexuals who do attention-grabbing things.

Author: The gays I have interviewed have said that sex is not the thing, that love is the thing, and that they have the same love feelings that everybody else has.

Chris: The thing with me is, that I love women as friends, but I could not live with a woman because of their character; and sexually I can't. I've already been with a woman once and I could not ejaculate; and physically I'm not attracted. Other than that, I just can't get along with them as I can a man. I love men. There is a physical bond of loving and holding and nurturing that you get from being close to a guy that I don't get from a girl, that I can't get from a girl, because I feel uncomfortable. If I hugged a woman, I could love her as a friend, but I could not have that same bonding feeling that I get with a man.

Chapter Sixteen

Weasel

Q: What age were you when you first realized that you were different?

A: I was thirteen to fourteen years old.

Q: What did you think about it?

A: I was relieved and glad to finally feel at ease with someone sexually and emotionally.

Q: How did you cope with it?

A: I didn't have any problems. My family were all very receptive. They stated that they thought that I was gay since I was a teenager.

Q: How did you handle yourself with the boy-girl issue?

A: When I was a kid I played with Barbies and dolls with my sister. But I had a *Barbie* and a *Ken* doll. I usually played with boys in my neighborhood when I was young. I didn't have very many girls that I played with. As I got older I usually had just one good friend (a girl) at a time, and I would totally focus on her.

Q: What kind of toys did you play with?

A: I played football, and baseball, and with trucks, and race cars. I also played with Barbies and Frisbees, stuffed animals and trading cards.

Q: How did the other kids and teachers in school treat you?

A: They didn't treat me any differently.

Q: How old were you when you came out?

A: I was twenty-four years old.

Q: Who was the first person that you "came out" to?

A: The first person that I told was my mother. I told my mom first because I am close to her. I wanted to share my happiness with her. I was in love, and I wanted her to know it. I live in California and she lives in Iowa, so I told her over the phone.

Q: How did she take it?

A: My mom was great. She said, "It's OK honey." (Because I was crying while trying to tell her). She told me that she and my sisters had thought that I was gay since I was a teenager.

Q: How did your siblings take it?

A: We all were very affectionate and got along fine.

Q: How did they treat you after they knew that you were gay?

A: They didn't treat me any differently. My sisters just ask me a lot of questions. They say they want to know everything.

Q: Do you have anything that you would like to share?

A: The first time my mom met my significant other she gave her a hug and welcomed her into the family with open arms.

Q: How does your family treat you now that you are grown?

A: Fine, loving, just the way they always did.

Q: How do your co-workers treat you on the job?

A: I am very lucky. All of my co-workers know that I am gay. I work in a large institution. My significant other works with me. People treat us great. There were a few people that we had trouble with at first. I think that is because they knew my significant other for a few years as a single mother. When I entered the picture, they saw me as a bad person in the relationship. But after they got to know me and the two of us together, they all accepted us and treated us fine. They actually get worried if they think we might be fighting.

Q: Are you in a permanent relationship?

A: Yes.

Q: Do you want children?

A: No. My significant other has a son, and we've been together almost six years, and so we've raised him together from age six to age thirteen.

Q: Do you consider yourself promiscuous?

A: No.

Q: Are you religious?

A: Yes, I am Catholic.

Q: How are you coping with life in a straight society?

A: It is not too bad. Since we live in California, it is easier. We are not young and promiscuous. We are in a permanent relationship, so we don't find too many restrictions. There are some things that upset me. Society does not give us, as a couple, the same breaks that they give to heterosexual couples, just because we are the same sex.

We are both professionals. We are homeowners. We own two homes. We are raising a child. We pay taxes, but we can't file together. We both have to carry benefits. It's so frustrating...

Q: Do you have any comments that you would like to share? Is there something you would like to say to the rest of the world?

A: I just wish that all of the people in this world who think Gays are freaks and don't deserve to live could see the way that the majority of Gays live and dress. The only ones they see are the outrageous ones who want to shock people and cause havoc. They are the ones who go on the talk shows. They get on the news and out in the gay pride parades, etc. The majority of us are hard-working, responsible professionals. We dress, eat, drive, and sleep the same way that heterosexuals do. Our only difference is that we are emotionally and sexually attracted to someone of the same sex. What I do in my bed is no one's business but my own. I don't beat my spouse or our son. I don't steal. I don't do drugs. I do everyday things like eat, work, play, do homework with our son and sleep. We are just like any other heterosexual couple out there.

CHAPTER SEVENTEEN

ALEXANDER

I first realized that I was Gay or different when I was about five years old. I was probably in the first grade. I know that at that time I was acutely aware that it was not appropriate for little boys to be attracted to other little boys. I was also aware that the other boys were already beginning to express negative feelings or words about what was then almost exclusively called queers or fags. It was always used in a derogatory manner to impugn someone's masculinity. It was difficult to cope with at that age, because I knew that I was not attracted to girls as were other boys. I knew that my feelings towards other boys were something that I could never discuss or express to anyone. It was easy for me to just smile politely when anyone would comment how someday I would be chasing the girls just like all boys were expected to when they grew up.

It was easy to pretend to be straight. It seemed easier than to have to deal with the fact of being gay in a straight world. When I was growing up in the late 1950's there was no such thing as the Gay Liberation Movement that we are all so aware of today. I wonder often how things might have been different for me if I were growing up in today's more open and enlightened world. Back then I only knew that I was different from the other boys. The Stonewall Riots that marked the beginning of the modern Gay Rights Movement didn't even occur until I was already sixteen years old. There was absolutely no anchor or touchstone that I could relate to as I was growing up Gay. It was an extremely lonely time in my life.

I think that I played with ordinary toys when I was young. I was interested in model trains, toy soldiers, toy cars, a stuffed animal or two, but not dolls in particular. In school I was the model student. My grades were always above average. The teachers all adored me because I was so well-behaved. I was smart enough to know how to handle the other boys and girls in school. I was adept at the art of becoming invisible. I was never that athletically skilled, although I enjoyed the occasional game of stick-ball on the block where I lived. I knew how to remain quiet when I was around the other kids, and more often than not they didn't notice me when I was around. Which is exactly the way I wanted it to be.

Throughout my life, and starting I would say when I was about five, I have always felt uncomfortable around straight boys or straight men. I have felt inadequate around what I will choose to call their easy, natural masculinity. It's not that I have necessarily felt feminine in their presence. It's just that I never possessed their characteristic macho-ism and propensity toward jock-like horseplay. I felt as though I was missing a certain gene or something that made guys act in the way that so many straight boys and men do. It's behavior that I always wished that I possessed. I felt that it would have made my life so much easier to be just one of the guys. There are many Gay men who possess that jock-like masculinity. It's not something that is the sole ability of straight boys and men. I look at those Gay men with the same sort of subtle envy as I do when I see straight men who act that way. Needless to say, I avoided all social events where sports were played. I could neither play the game nor act like the tough guy in the stands rooting for his team. That sense of being different led to further isolation from people my own age, and people in general. My reputation from childhood to young adult could be simply summed up as the smart, quiet, nice guy.

MY ADOLESCENCE

I was approximately 22 years old when I "came out." The first person that I told that I was Gay was my friend Jeff, who I already knew was gay himself. I know that I told Jeff first because it would be easier than anyone in my family or my other friends. I also liked Jeff as a person. We are still good, close friends to this very day. Some 20 years later, I have never had the experience of telling my father that I was gay, although I know that he knew. I did, however, tell my mother in a face to face talk. I had the opportunity to do this about a year after I came out to Jeff. I suppose I did this at that time in my life because I began to feel more comfortable about my own sexuality, and the fact that it had already been about a year since I had come out to Jeff. I knew that my mother was becoming anxious about the issue of my sexuality. I knew that she strongly suspected, and I was having a lot of fun at the bars at that time, and was starting to date. I didn't want to play the charade any longer. One afternoon during a confrontational conversation she asked me if I were gay, and I said yes. She took the news with a sense of shock and spent the afternoon crying bitterly. To say the least, it was an unpleasant experience for me. I was nonetheless relieved that the truth had finally come out.

As far as my other family members and relatives are concerned, I can sum up my entire experience with them. Of my being gay... As follows...it has never been discussed with any of them. They simply ignore the issue, and I intuitively know that it is a topic not to be brought up. Of course, I wish that the situation could have been different. But I always knew that they would respond like that. So to me it seems perfectly normal behavior on their part. Throughout my entire life, none of my family members and I have ever discussed my being Gay, except for that one time with my mother.

ADULTHOOD

My family has treated me well my entire life. Their only oddity is the fact that my being gay is never discussed in any way. It's a subtle form of disapproval, and I do not resent them for doing it. I feel that they are only responding as best they know how. Aside from that, my relationship with them is very good.

I have always worked in gay-oriented businesses or, I should say, places where being gay was not an issue. I'm referring to my work in hair salons and in restaurants (as a waiter). I never had any problem with co-workers because I was Gay, even though there are many other straight employees in these businesses. I think it's because the straight employees in these businesses realized that there were many gay people in these fields, and just accepted it as the way things were. I think that to some extent I may have consciously chosen these fields because I, too, knew that there were many Gay people who worked in them. I do know I definitely avoided fields of work where I may have thought that Gays were routinely treated with hostility, such as the military and the teaching profession.

I am not in a permanent type relationship now, nor have I been for the past ten years, although I most definitely would like to be. During most of these ten years I felt that I was not capable of being in a relationship, and therefore avoided one at all costs. I felt that I needed to be on a quest of personal discovery, to find out who I really was. I needed to find out how and why I behaved the way that I did in the two live-in relationships that I did have in the past. Also to find out why they both went so terribly sour. I feel that through years of reading and counseling that I have discovered many new insights into myself and am once again ready to reenter the relationship scene. I am looking forward to that time with eagerness.

Yes, I definitely would like to have children someday. I don't think, however, that is a situation that I will ultimately be ready for; for a number of reasons. At 41, I feel that I am just now beginning to know myself. In many ways I feel more like 21 than 41. Children are a tremendous emotional and financial responsibility. Up until now I have not been secure in either one of these areas. I think that I would prefer to adopt a child rather than have one of my own. I don't feel the overwhelming need to have a child of my own when there are so many children in the world in need of a loving home.

I don't consider myself to be religious in the traditional sense. I do, however, give thanks every day in my daily prayers. I don't go to Mass on a regular basis. I generally am not a follower of the Catholic faith, even though I was raised as one. I think that the Pope's stand on homosexuality turns me off to the church in general. I have, however, gone to the St. Thomas Episcopal Church in Manhattan on many occasions, and have felt much more accepted there, for reasons that I don't entirely understand. I don't feel that the Episcopal Church has the same anti-gay stance as the Catholic Church. I suppose that is why I feel more comfortable there.

The way I have chosen to cope with life in a straight society, is not to live in one. I recently moved to the West Hollywood area and have never been happier in my entire life. Don't get me wrong, I have nothing against straight society. It's just that I don't feel entirely comfortable there. It's like the feeling of being the only black person in a room full of white people. I just feel so comfortable in West Hollywood that I wish I had moved here many years ago. It's such a nice feeling to see so many Gay-owned and oriented establishments, where a person can feel as validated as straight people do in their own society. I really have not had any special problems in straight society. I think that is because of my conservative appearance and manner. I mentioned earlier that very early in life I learned the ability of how to become invisible and silent. That is a characteristic that has helped me to avoid troublesome situations throughout my life. I do think that I would have become a much more extroverted type of person had I not had to deal with being Gay in a world where being Gay was not at all acceptable. Living in West Hollywood will give me the opportunity to open up that part of myself that I've suppressed for so long. It will be a slow process, akin to ice melting after a long winter. I, nevertheless, look forward to the spring.

CONCLUSION

I am optimistic that in time the Gay Rights Movement will erode the long held barriers and prejudices that the world has held onto for so long. I do not resent the world for their anti-gay actions. I just feel that they do not know any better and, in time, they may come to a new level of understanding. I think that it will be through books such as yours that will contribute to this process of understanding. For that, I deeply thank you for your courage and wisdom. I am grateful that I live in a time and in a place where being Gay no longer carries the stigma that it once did. Of course, we have a long way to go before gaining full acceptance and equality. I like to give thanks for those things that I do have and am blessed with, rather than concentrate on what I believe I do not have. In many ways I consider myself to be a very fortunate person.

CHAPTER EIGHTEEN

SETH'S STORY

Seth: Well, first off, I didn't know what homosexual or gay was. But I can remember that I always had an attraction for guys as far back as before kindergarten. At least I remember playing with the other kids on the street, you know — doctor. I always wanted to play with dolls, play house and office. But also I liked Tonka trucks and Hot Wheels. My older cousin and a couple of his friends used to make me do things that I actually began to like. That's when I began *discovering*. That was actually fourth or fifth grade. My cousins — they are not gay. I guess they were just going through an experimental stage. I remember in fifth grade that I had a crush on a girl. I thought she was just the prettiest thing. But she didn't like me. In sixth grade I did have a girlfriend. But she was just a friend. I never kissed her. I never did anything like that. In seventh grade, I had a crush on a girl named Shannon who I just adored. Seventh grade is probably where I started getting screwed up. Because she liked this guy named Victor. And I also liked Victor! *A lot!* That is the same year that I went through the rape. I believe that's when life started getting very difficult. My mom and dad were going through a divorce. He's not my biological father, but he married my mom right before I was born.

Author: What about the rape? Who did it?

Seth: I was in the seventh grade, so I was about twelve. I was going to a Christian private school. He was the principal. He was also the pastor to the church. That was a very *Traumatic-Traumatic* experience for me. I trusted him implicitly. He had become a father figure. I was having a very difficult time at home. My mom was newly married to my new stepfather and I was having a hard time with that. During that period I began to

106

notice that I liked boys a lot more. He [the principal] started giving me special treatment. If we ever went to football games, or anything with the school, he always had me ride with him. He called my mother and asked her if he could take me to a movie. Of course, she said yes, because he was a respected person. After the movie, he took me home the long way. He violated me very brutally. I still haven't recovered from it, to be perfectly honest with you. I still have nightmares. At that time I felt so betrayed that I didn't trust men, period. Not my previous stepfather, not my new stepfather, not my uncle. Nobody. I couldn't. I felt so betrayed. I cried forever.

I was a very emotional person at one time. I didn't know what was the matter with me. I also didn't understand why I was having attraction for boys. I liked a girl and…I liked the boy that she liked… What a soap opera. This was the beginning of the eighties and this had a horrendous influence on me. You know Soft Cell and Depeche Mode and Boy George, because of the type of music they played and the way they dressed. Everybody was wearing make-up. I saw all these guys on television who were stars, who were wearing tons of makeup, and looked like women. And I thought, oh I like it! I used to run around in my mom's high heels. I loved it! I just loved it! I played dress up whenever I could get away with it.

Author: Did you tell your mother about the rape?

Seth: To be honest with you, I never told her the entire story until I was about seventeen years old. I had come home the night of the ordeal, a terrible disaster. I was crying uncontrollably. I only told her bits and pieces of it. What she did was, go down to the school and talk to him. He said he was sorry, and she didn't press charges, she just didn't do anything. I felt like everything was brushed under the rug. When I finally did tell her the entire story, she was very, very upset. That made her understand why I was going through so much trauma. I felt that the night of my ordeal was when I lost my innocence altogether, and I believe that has controlled a big part of my life since. A lot of people have been molested. But mine was a more serious molestation.

Author: [The more lurid details have been omitted for reasons of privacy.]

Seth: It was a very brutal rape. He threatened me with my life. He had a gun. He finally got caught. There were seven others in my school. When something like this happens, it completely destroys your trust in anyone you previously thought you could trust. Who can I trust now? No one.

Author: What age were you when you first told your mother that you were a homosexual?

Seth: Mom figured it out. There was a show on television called "Joanie Loves Chachi." I totally loved this show, and she asked me was it because you love Joanie, or is it because you love Chachi? At the time, of course, I obviously said Joanie. But I had always had a crush on Chachi. One of the most difficult people that I had to confront and tell was my mother. I was probably about sixteen. I had fully "come out" at that time except to her. I came out full blown at fourteen to all of my friends. By that time I knew exactly what I was. When I was sixteen my stepfather found out and wanted to send me to see a priest, to get me fixed up, because he's Catholic. I wouldn't do it, so he turned me out of his house. My grandmother came to the rescue. Thank God for my grandmother. I stayed with her for a short time. Then my mother came to get me. I told her the whole thing. I told her the whole story about the rape. That's when she told me about my stepfather not being my biological father. We talked about my being Gay. It was a very emotional day needless to say. Very, very emotional day. When I came out, I did it very wrong. Because when I came out, I shoved it into everybody's face and said accept it... deal with it... live with it... and get over it... That was wrong.

Author: It's so "kid." It's what a child would do. You're not alone. This is how a kid deals with things that they are stressed and angry about. They don't know how to be diplomatic. You don't learn diplomacy until you get a lot of mileage on you.

Seth: My grandmother is really great about it, and my mother is...well she's fine about it. She has met people I've gone out with. She's met all my gay friends. She's allowed me to bring a person I'm seeing into her home. She knows I'm very respectful, and very tactful, and I would never do anything to disrespect her or her home. I never have, and I never will, and so she respects me. My stepfather and I, we don't ever talk any more. Our relationship has never been the same since he found out.

Author: When your mother first found out, how did she take it?

Seth: She cried-cried-cried! She was angry. She thought it was her. It was all her fault. Which I think is something that a lot of mothers have to go through. Then eventually, hopefully, like you did, and like my mother did, they finally realize that it wasn't them at all. *It's not the parents fault.* Her most difficult thing to deal with was the fact that I'm the only child. She wanted to have grandchildren. She wanted me to be happy. She knew I've always had a miserable life. Another thing that makes me somewhat different than perhaps 90% of homosexuals, is that I have never had sex with a woman. Never had the desire to try it.

Author: You did tell me that you tried it and that it didn't work.

Seth: To be blunt, I got as far as my boxers, and I said uh-uh, the energy is just not there. It's not going to work. I was repulsed! And that's when I knew for sure. I didn't want this. I wanted the football players and the polo players. That's what I wanted. In high school I dated a pretty girl, she was the cheerleader. That was my freshman year. She was history by the end of my freshman year. All girls, period, were history. I just wanted to keep them as friends.

Author: What about the rest of your family when you came out? Your cousins, etc.

Seth: Of my cousins that I grew up with, the oldest never had a problem with it. The middle one didn't have a problem with it for a long time. Then something happened with him, and he all of a sudden turned against me. Most of their friends, and everyone else that I grew up with, turned against me. Then my mom's side, the cousins, started turning on me. I'm not allowed to be around any of the younger ones. At least that's the way it was a couple of years ago. That hurt a lot. They feel that they have to keep an eye on me, if I were around the younger ones, because they thought I was going to do something. I tried to explain to them, "Why would I do something to them that was done to me." I guess they didn't comprehend it. I have a lot of anger and resentment toward them. It is very unforgivable as far as I'm concerned. I just don't think it's going to change anytime soon.

Author: Do you think they rejected you out of their religious beliefs?

Seth: Yes, I believe that had something to do with it. I thought, that's right, you just preach to me about your religion that does nice things only for people who give the most money.

Author: When you were with your grandmother you told me that you attempted to commit suicide. How old were you then?

Seth: I was pretty close to eighteen. It was right after Easter. The whole family had gotten together at some property up in the mountains. My stepmother and one of the aunts had gone around and told the rest of the family on my mom and dad's side that I was gay. A lot of them, to this day, still won't have anything to do with me. I felt that was the straw that broke the camel's back. I had never gotten along with my stepmother. I just couldn't take it anymore. I wasn't getting along with my mom or step-mom. I was even starting to fight with my grandmother.

I just felt as if I had lost everything. Little did I know that life was going to be many, many UPS and many, many DOWNS, and so I *tried.*

Author: You did a pretty good job of it...

Seth: Yes, I did actually. I cut my wrists. After it was already done, I decided that I didn't want to die. But that's something that I still deal with until this day. You know suicide... Because there are sometimes that I get so out of it. I feel I've had enough. I try... I always fight with those little demons that I've always had.

Author: Do you envision your life taking this tack? (Someday I will meet the right person — fall in love — and settle down and establish a home and make a commitment for life?)

Seth: Yes! Yes I do! I believe in the whole marriage thing. Eventually I'm going to start dating again. It's like my mother used to say, play the field... But in our life that usually means having sex with every person that you date. And I don't want to be like that. *At all.* I lost that a long time ago.

Author: I think, with a lot of people the scenario kind of goes like this: You meet a person and you have expectations. You're attracted, you get something going, it falls through, and they leave you for someone else. This hurts you over and over again. That's why it's not a good thing to get physically involved. I think that's why God never intended for us to be too easy and too ready to jump into things. Because we're open for so much hurt. And hurt damages your inner soul.

Because we're so vulnerable.

Seth: See, I don't do that now. My reason is simply because I don't trust them. I'm not the type of person to give myself 100% to anybody. I've made a lot of mistakes. We expect to be accepted throughout society, as human beings, as people, and to be just like everybody else. Everybody wants to go out to the bars and have the night life, which I did. You can go out every single night, you know, and have your "one night stands." It doesn't hurt you because you don't love. It doesn't hurt. You put the shell out. Because all you are doing is just giving them shell. And it's nothing. It doesn't mean anything. I was just as bad. I was a West Hollywood clone a long time ago. But it's not like that now.

Author: You know, you should join a gay support group here in your area. In Orange County they have a group. It's under the auspices of the Catholic Church. They are outreaching to the gay community. There are people of all ages. Many of them have been in the closet most of their lives. They lived celibate lives. Some of them entered the priesthood or the convent, thinking that was the only thing that they could do. And they are wonderful, down-to-earth people. All of these people are lonely. They are searching. Every one of them, even the old grandmas, couldn't tell their families because they knew they would be rejected. They are struggling through life, trying to come to grips with what they are. And how they are going to live their lives. You need to join a group like this, where there are people you can get with and talk to.

Seth: When I was trying to talk with my mother about it years ago she said, "You had it easy, you never went without, you always had a roof over your head, and food in your stomach." But that wasn't it... She didn't grow up... Me. I had a really rough time, and I wouldn't live it over. That's for sure. I have always hated my life. I have always been a very unhappy person.

It's just difficult to try to find all the answers and know which way to go. I've been trying to get all of the bad people out of my life. I just don't want to live like this any more. That's why so many of us commit suicide. The last thing that we need is for our parents to turn on us. I think my mom finally realized that. I always thought of her side of the family as being such strong religious people but they weren't perfect.

My grandmother, on my mom's side, found out that my uncle, to this day, has homosexual tendencies. He had also gone through a lot of the things that I have gone through. But he's married and has two kids, and now has to deal with the fact that he still has these tendencies. The family is not so perfect after all. When I was really vulnerable and hurt I needed them so much. They weren't there. Now that they are realizing that there is somebody else in the family who is having a difficult time now, and is in his forties, and has a wife and two kids, and is struggling, they try to come to me for some kind of an answer. *I* knew that *I* wasn't supposed to get married to a woman and have children that way. My aunt, she's going through a really difficult time. She knows everything that's going on. She's been a very strong person for him. But eventually something is going to give. Because it is something that is never going to go away. YOU EITHER ARE OR YOU AREN'T. It's very simple. He had a rough childhood as well. And as far as I'm concerned, it's too late. I needed them when I was younger, and they weren't there. That's why, I think, I've been through a lot of different people. I mean a lot of boyfriends and everything, because I was looking for — searching for — you know — love — that I felt that I never got before. I just believe that I have turned out the way that I am because of all the past.

Author: From your own hurt?

Seth: Yes, exactly! I don't go out of my way to lead a destructive life. I just don't know exactly how to change it.

Author: You're getting tired of it, yourself?

Seth: Oh, my gosh, yes, ever since I've been out on my own. Even before that. I'm tired of going through relationships. You know, homosexuals are real people. They grow up looking for love. The same kind of love that everybody else is looking for.

Someone to be there for them. I think that's the reason why a lot of us do go out to the sex clubs, like the ones that we have here in Los Angeles. There's one here... I did not know that it was a sex club. My friend and I heard that it was a disco type place. It was brand new, so we went over to check it out... (He draws his breath in and covers his face in a shocked gesture.) Aaahhh!!! You pay twelve bucks to get in. I'm telling you. I have never in my life. It was worse than a porno. I think a lot of people do that because in a way, it's to look for acceptance. Because it's some type of love. I don't think it's just because of being a whore, or a slut. When I discovered what it was, well my friend and I were like locked together, walking around. And this place looks like a dungeon. We were just going...aawwwaaahhh... We were there probably a good half hour, going around the whole place because it's large. I mean two story. THESE PEOPLE... I've never seen that before. It was a good experience (he gets serious). I'm not a voyeur. I would never do anything like that. I mean like participate in something like that. We went — we saw — we left...and I've seen some things. But I never saw anything like that. It was an experience.

Author: [Even though this young man has been "out" since a very young age and has not had the benefit of a solid Christian education, he is still a decent human being and has no desire to be blatantly immoral.]

Seth: I don't believe that there is anybody here, in this area, or a homosexual — period — who would ever choose, necessarily, to ever be a homosexual. Because of the fact that it is a very lonely lifestyle. To live in a society where you are basically a social outcast... It's difficult to be this way. You can't just CHOOSE to be gay. I mean — WHY WOULD YOU? Why would anyone choose to be quote, unquote, a social outcast? To live a lonely lifestyle? Always looking for some type of acceptance. If we don't get it from the outside society, we are always looking for it within our own society. It's really difficult. Especially in West Hollywood. All in all, it's a very lonely lifestyle. You're very unsure of yourself you know. A lot of people can't handle it, and that's why they commit suicide. When you are dealing with an HIV status, you are even more alone. *But why would a person choose to be gay if a person could choose to be straight?? To be* part of the rest of the world? Yes exactly! It's why I think we are striving for so much acceptance here. We have realized that we are human beings. We didn't wake up one morning, and turn on a light switch, and say: HEY, I'M GAY. This is the way we have *always* been. We deserve the right to feel loved and be loved, and have a normal working environment, and a normal lifestyle, like heterosexuals. You know, we deserve the same thing. I don't believe that we deserve any special privileges. There are a few groups out there — they really go overboard — they're militant. Like ACT UP, for example. And sometimes I believe that causes us more harm than good.

Author: I believe that homosexual and heterosexuals should all be the same and have the same rules. Your mom and dad tell you when you are a little kid, *"Don't sleep around, wait until you get married because you're not supposed to do that."* Kids grow up, they date people, and they make mistakes. They will fall *in* love, and *out of* love until they find the right one. I've interviewed people who were together for years. Then it just went wrong. They didn't get married, but their *intention* was to do the right thing. Even though celibacy is the right thing to do, and the ideal, it is not always what is actually happening. Statistics are showing us this. But this is the rule that everyone lives by. If they do fail and sleep with someone they think, "Well, that was a mistake, I won't do that again, I'll wait." And this is the social ethic of all heterosexual people today. Homosexuals should not behave any differently than heterosexuals. They should try to be decent and *not* go around to the bath houses, etc. In other words, don't deliberately be promiscuous. *We should all have the same rules because we all have the same GOD.* GOD never said I have one set of rules for some of My people and another set for a different group of people. I think HE meant *all* of His rules for *all* His people. We all have the same heaven, we all have the same sins, we all have the same Hell to avoid. For too long gays have been given no rules and it has gotten out of hand. It's not their fault, because no one has given them any consideration or evangelization. Gays should be accepted as regular people and they should live like heterosexuals, and date the same way, and make the same mistakes, and all have the same intentions, and we should all be the same community of souls.

Author: Do you want to meet someone and make a commitment?

Seth: Yes. Oh Yeah! See!... This is what I want. I want to get married some day. And I want to get married once. *That's it!* I think that's why so many of us go through so many relationships. Because we are trying to find that happiness and inner peace for ourselves.

I myself have gone through so many relationships, because I was looking for a lot of things that I just couldn't find. The relationships always ended up...ending.

See, I have a lot of open wounds from my childhood that I've not closed yet. Wounds that I need to heal before I ever get involved with somebody again. I contacted my natural father! I traced him down through my mom. She told me the name of my natural grandmother. And I talked her into giving me the name of my father and his phone number. So I could call him... And... (His voice drops to a whisper...) He rejected me. He said, he didn't want anything to do with me... (He looks away, and his eyes fill with tears...)

Author: Seth had always fantasized, ever since he found out that he had a natural father, that his *real* father would (maybe) love him. I guess he was wrong.

CHAPTER NINETEEN

ALLEN'S STORY

Author: What age were you when you first realized that you were different?

Allen: I was about five years old, at least by five. I pretty much knew what was going on. By ten or eleven I had researched the whole thing and I knew what was happening. Both of my parents were teachers and we had an enormous book collection. Biology books were very freely available in our household. I knew body parts and I knew what was going on. I had already looked up the term homosexuality, and I knew where my thinking was. I was always different. I fit in OK, but I was always on the fringe. I had lots of friends, both boy friends and girl friends who I played with. I was always digging forts, building stuff, and falling out of tree houses. However, I always knew that there was something a little bit different about life somewhere.

As far as growing up I did all the things that one would traditionally do as a boy growing up. It wasn't really different. I just knew that I was different. I don't know that I was picked on any more than anyone else who was a little bit different. There is no way of getting around that. If you are different, you are going to be subjected to it. I had a more creative bent and so that automatically makes you stand out. I was always involved in some sort of art work. I was a better builder than anybody else. I learned early how to use a hammer and nails, and I was sought out for that.

Author: What age were you when you first came out?

Allen: I was about fourteen or fifteen. I already knew in my mind what was going on. I had a girlfriend for school purposes, but I was also dating two other guys at the same time. I had already experimented, so everything kind of fell into place.

I was sixteen when I first told my parents. Initially my mother was pretty upset over the whole thing.

Author: You told me that your mother wanted to jump out of the car. Do you want to tell me about that incident?

Allen: We were driving in the car, on the freeway, and I just decided that this would be the appropriate time to tell her for sure. I already figured that she suspected. My father knew and had already dealt with it. But my mom didn't know. So I just blurted it out. I said this is how it is, take it or leave it. And she kind of wanted to fling herself out of the car at that point, with all of the guilt and all of the typical mother stuff. Once she settled down, she looked at it realistically. We talked about it and we talked very openly. They were very open people. Being teachers, both of my parents were well-educated. I guess it was kind of a shock at first. I don't remember it being any big deal after she calmed down. There were tears, of course, over some period of time.

They took me to a psychiatrist. After two sessions the psychiatrist told them I was fine. So they said, "Let's deal with it from that point." I never remember any negative feelings toward it. If they had not been as well-educated as they were, perhaps things might have been different. Also they had known gay people in their lives. I don't ever remember it being like the horror stories that I have heard about other people going through. Once they did the psychiatrist thing, they decide that everything was fine and dandy. From that point on it was never an issue.

Author: Were you closer to your mom or your dad?

Allen: Oh, definitely my mom. There was no doubt about it. My father was also a typical "Fifties" father. "Fifties" fathers just didn't do a lot of socializing with their kids. He was like any other father of that era. He was great. He taught me how to ski, and build, and how to do gymnastics. We lived for years in Sequoia National Park, so we fished and backpacked.

He taught me to do all of that stuff. But as far as being demonstrative with affection, dads of the "Fifties" just didn't do that. My mom was a homemaker, so when she was home I had more interaction with her. He took it about the way that any man would take the situation. I think it took him longer to get used to the idea. I guess that part of it was really hard for me because I was already comfortable with the notion. I just sort of told him. When we sat and talked about it they kind of knew that they each had to deal with it. They were very widely traveled. I think that my grandmother was helpful in that. She was supportive, and for a woman of her era, she was well-educated and extremely well-traveled. She had been around all kinds of people in her early years. I think a lot of that is what really helped me. I think that the reason that I have maintained two very long term relationships is that from day one I had a lot of familial support.

I have two brothers. One is a year and a half younger and one is five years younger. My little brother is also gay. When he made the final announcement, we all knew he was. Was he more effeminate? Actually no, in fact he's a real charmer. He walks into a room and all of the women flock to him. He is completely opposite from me. His idea of a long term relationship is two days. We were raised basically the same. My other brother who was raised in the same household is straight. He's a lumberjack type of person. He has no problems with my relationships. His wife comes down and stays with us every year for the holidays. We go to their house and we are accepted as a couple. When my straight brother was engaged to his wife, he decided to bring her down and introduce her to the family. I like to cook and have family dinners. My mother does not cook. She does not do the typical mother stuff. When he decided to bring her down and introduce her to the family, it was for Thanksgiving.

In my parent's house the family traveled over the holidays. I used to have to spend Christmas with whoever was available from work. They would be up skiing for the entire week, and I wouldn't see them until after Christmas. When I got a home of my own, I started the tradition of an open door. I swore that there would never be anyone who would have to go to a restaurant for the holiday. Everyone knows that I cook dinner, and if they don't have any place to go, my house will always be open. My brother knew this very intimately when he brought her down. This poor woman was subjected to this household of about twenty-five to thirty-five people and only three of us were family. The rest of them were all hanger-oners who were sitting down to this meal with food fights and conversations going all over the place. She survived that. Not only did she fit in, but she said that she had a good time. I said, "That's fine, she'll work, it will be great." Within our family unit, it's always been whoever wants to, has just come in. If my brother was dating someone, they were just included. My nephews have grown up since day one knowing that they have two uncles who live together. They refers to both of us as their uncles. They don't even question it. My brother has been very open about our relationship. Now that my little brother is in the latter stages of AIDS, my nephews are both acquainted with that. They have never denied anything about it. When they come down to visit their Uncle Ralph, they know that he is dying. The family has been very open about that. From day one my little brother told us that he was HIV positive. We kind of all assumed that he was, just because of his lifestyle. He's known he's positive since eighteen. He's at that stage where he's sick more of the time than well. The families feeling has been, "OK, we'll deal with it." There was never any condemnation. We've lost so many friends, at this point that it has just become a fact of life.

High school is probably the hardest time of all when it comes to younger years and growing up years. Because I make no bones about it, I'm effeminate. I know that I am. I always have been. I mean, I love all the masculine stuff. There just isn't anything you can do about what God gave you. You learn to deal with it, and in many respects it made me stronger. I learned how to fight early, because if somebody is going to beat me up for being a sissy, I had to learn how to fight·back. I'm definitely a survivor. There is no sling or arrow or barb that you can throw that I can't defend myself against. I'm not going to break down and cry and run away. I think that's the reason that many gay people are as successful as they are. Because we survive or die. You have no options. You learn these lessons early. It creates a scenario where it forces us to be successful. We know we have to be. Coming out in the years that I did, there weren't the support groups that there 'are now. There was basically nothing but bars to go to. There weren't any Gay and Lesbian community centers. Or religious groups, or bowling leagues or all the stuff that there is today. I look back now on some of the things that I did, and I wonder, how did I survive? I would never do some of the things now that I did then.

Aside from the issue of AIDS, I think it is probably a lot better now. I haven't been out in the dating world for so long I can hardly remember what it was like. There are just a lot more options now. To have to go through what I had to go through in the early years, I wouldn't wish it on my worst enemy. When you hear people talking about it as, *"This is a choice that you have made."* I look at them and I think, "In the first place, I am not suicidal." If I thought this was a choice, why would I subject myself to the kinds of things that I've done simply to find out who I am. Why would any rational person in their right mind go out and take the chances that I have, because those are the only options.

I learned how to get into bars at sixteen because I made friends with the doorman. I knew that was the only way to get past that door and to have someone there to protect me if I got into trouble. I was young, I was nice looking, I was thin, I was sixteen to seventeen years old, and I could get into Disneyland for under twelve. So I was pretty fair game. You found out what this world was like because you had no where else to go. There were no teachers. There were no people to school you. I had no priest to go to. I had absolutely no one to turn to, to find out what these feelings were about. So those years were very difficult. A lot of mistakes were made. A lot of them I wouldn't wish on my worst enemy. I was sneaking around, driving into Los Angeles because it was the only place to go, and standing on the side of a street in the middle of the night. What sixteen year old person in their right mind would drive into an unfamiliar area by themselves and stand on a street just to meet someone who is like themselves? If you really look at it, is that a choice? I don't think so.

Now in this day and age there are places to go to, so I think it's a lot safer. Barring the issue of AIDS, in those times there were a lot of my friends who didn't survive. I knew about drug overdoses before I wanted to. Simply because it was a way to make life seem better. There was a great deal of pain to get over. If it hadn't been for the fact of my family, and how supportive they were, I probably would have been one of the drugsters. I took my share. There wasn't one that went by that I didn't try. It was the Sixties and my whole world had been turned upside down. So you develop skills. I have learned a lot about people, and I use it every day. I know how to communicate. I know that somebody always has to answer to somebody. I learned to really respect people. Not look down on them. In the Gay world you meet people from all walks of life, because the community is relatively small.

You count your friends from among all of these people. I think it's a wonderful education. So instead of living on the pain of what happened in some of those early years, I chose to see it as a learning experience, and gather from it. Lots of people didn't look at it that way. They chose to see it as a painful lesson rather than a learning lesson.

Author: How did you meet your partner?

Allen: Basically I've had two long term relationships. One that lasted about eight years. And this one, going on seventeen now. The first one I met at a party. He was the ultimate athlete, a member of the Dodgers Farm Team, police officer, extremely good looking, and extremely abusive. As I approached adulthood in my late twenties, and he was seeing me getting older. I think it affected him. He became even more abusive. Finally, I got smart enough to say, "This is really stupid, why am I taking this?" It was a pretty nasty separation.

I met the person that I am with now in a bar. I was still coming out of the first relationship. So I wanted to spend some time on my own. So I told him up front, "If you want to be around in a couple of years, fine we can date. But I'm doing stuff that I need to do for me." So the dating process began. We dated for almost three years, which I fully advise as the only way to go. Date — don't live with them. It's just like any engagement, or any kind of relationship, when you learn about the person. We traveled together quite a bit. We went places together on the weekends. We maintained separate residences. I was allowed my space to do what I needed to do. Because he was older and a professional person, we also worked through a lot of the issues. Budget differences. Earning income differences. One of the things between male relationships is that social kind of competitiveness. There was a considerable difference in earning capacity, and there was the age difference.

I suffered quite a bit of suspicion as the gold digger, so we decided we would just take time to make sure that what we were doing was right. So we just maintained separate places and took time to pull it together. We took a long time before we ever lived under the same roof. It was the best thing that ever happened.

I stopped working and decided to stay home for awhile. We remodeled our house. All of a sudden I wasn't working, and I had always worked. Of the many gay couples that we see now in our world, one or the other partner has chosen to be secondary. Not to defame the women's movement, but I think that a household runs when a household is run well. I don't see it as being equal or unequal. I think there are a lot of women in the women's movement who have lost the idea that they can be valuable at home. In our relationship we kind of crossed that barrier a few years ago. How much money do we really need if all we are doing is working? So many of our friends have done what we have done. I have only worked part time for probably ten years. I work about a hundred hours doing any number of things around the house, and I don't have a problem with that. I feel very sorry for women who do have a problem with that; I think they miss out on a lot of what could be done if they felt they would be valuable at home.

A few years ago my other half needed an office manager. So I went in and started running his office. That was a struggle, trying to live together, and trying to work together. To do that took some major changes in our relationship. We had a lot of fights over how one ran things. My style of running an office was much different than his was. There was a lot to come to grips with. For him to back off and let me do what I do. That took some time. Over the years we have crossed a number of barriers and had a lot of fun with it. So it seems to be working.

Author: Are you a very religious person?

Allen: I personally grew up with very little organized religion. My parents were very big on appreciating nature. We lived in the Sierras most of my growing up years. My father said that their way of communing with God was getting out and hiking. My form of religion was to appreciate what was around me. My father had a disdain for anything that was organized, so I grew up with that. Spiritual, yes. Organized, no. My other half grew up multi-generational Seventh Day Adventist. He went through all the Adventist school system. So we both have a very strong spiritual background, and appreciate that within our relationship.

We are very involved in a group that is like *Dignity,* and any number of religious groups. It's called *Kinship.* Basically it's a support group for Gays and Lesbians. We've been heavy financial contributors over the years to the operation. We don't necessarily go to church every Sabbath but we are very involved. *Kinship* is not necessarily supported by the church. We've been in legal battles with them. We do have an underground following within the organizational corporate structure of the church. On the grass roots level and on the corporate level we have quite a bit of support. It has taken us about twenty years of being in operation to gather that type of support.

We do a camp meeting every year. We have a conference that we hold on either coast. We alternate. It is a week-long conference. Not only is it a time for our group, because it's a small group, it's over the whole United States and around the world. We don't have the option for everybody to see each other all the time. It's not like an organized type of Saturday worship. We use the yearly conference as a way to give everybody a connection with the other people so that they know that there's more out there. We also use it as a training ground for interested members of the organizational clergy.

We invite anywhere from a half a dozen to a dozen people from all levels of the structure of the church: educators, pastors, and people who are part of the actual corporate worldwide structure of the church. We use that as a time to educate them, and for them to see that we are not some pariah to be dealt with.

One of the best experiences that we have ever had over the years was probably four or five years ago. There's not necessarily a theme for the people who come to this particular camp meeting. Most of the clergy that were there were historians or religious ethicists dealing with texts out of the Bible etc. So for some reason they had a real "thing" on ethics. How the church really could not deal with us because they have this ethical issue. We were asking if they have pastors who would minister to us in a legitimate way. They said, "We can't do that because you are promiscuous and because you have all of these things, we gather, that don't agree with our ethics." There are a number of us who have been together for any number of years. At that particular camp meeting there was one couple who had been together for about 30 years. Another one for about 20 years. At that point my other half and I had been together for about ten or twelve years, and we were the youngsters of the group. So we thought about it amongst ourselves. We said, "Here's all of these people who say that they cannot give us their support because we are not adhering to the tenets of the church." We happened to look around at each other and said, "We are all in monogamous relationships. We have been in these relationships for years. We have adhered to every tenet that the church has professed. Why can't they give us the same thing?" So we went around and we got all of these couples together. We put them into a room. Unbeknownst to the rest of these clergy people, we brought all of them into the room. We sat all of them down, into a panel.

Then we said — NOW — "We have a question for you guys. All of these couples here have been together for "x" number of years. We all live in monogamous relationships. We all attend church on a fairly regular basis. We all believe in the same system. We all have some familial support within our families... YET... Why will you not minister to us if we have a marital problem? Do you have an issue with that? If we, between ourselves, are having what we would consider a marital problem, the same as any straight couple that came to you, would you not counsel us? If we are living the same exact lifestyle, why then will you not give us the same exact information that you would give this straight couple?" All of them, to a person, sat there and said, "Well... We don't know — because we are not prepared for you guys. We were prepared for the myths...and we could confront the myths... But now that we have been confronted with this situation, we have to think about our position..." It sat them back... Here were some people with an immense amount of education who were all-of-a-sudden going, "OH... OK... Now... we have to re-think this now because these people are doing what we are asking." Then we said, "You are misinformed. You have just told us why you can't minister to us. Now here are these people who are living according to the rules. They are not doing anything that they are not supposed to do. Do you have a problem with it?" Well, they had to sit back to think about it, and they did. It changed the whole tone of that camp meeting. All of a sudden then they were faced with dealing with us one-on-one in a much different way. That was a very important camp meeting. We are still dialoguing and having yearly get-togethers.

The Adventist church is very good on getting everyone to sing. I mean I couldn't hold a note in a bucket if I tried. So I am continually awed by the amount of talent that we get at the camp. I can't remember actually anyone over the years now, of the clergy, leaving and not having been tremendously and emotionally touched by the caring and the interaction. I have any number of them, when they leave, come up and say to us, "You know, if our regular churches could be like this, we would have finally gotten a grip on what the Bible was telling us, on what God was about. You guys let anybody come in. You let anybody worship in your place. Wherever you are, you have created a house of worship, which is exactly what the Bible says." You know we will set up logs in an area outside and hold the worship service outside. It is every bit as meaningful as sitting in a ten million-dollar church. We don't discriminate against anyone. We allow straight people to come in our church, and they get to be with us on the same level as anybody else. Whereas their churches won't let us come in and be on the same level. Any number of times we have been approached by these people who are pastors in their own churches. They have said, "If I could make my church be like yours, we would truly have a church." I have heard that so many times.

I think that straight society could learn from the gay community about learning to live together. Unlike the straight society, we don't have families. What happens to us when we get old? We have learned over the years to take care of ourselves. If you go out into the older gay community, you will almost always see a younger gay couple who takes on the older man whose partner of 25 years has died. He needs help. You see interesting complex family situations.

Extended family situations. It would not occur to me not to take someone in who needed help at a particular point in time. So you see dynamics of gay relationships are always interesting to look at. We don't have those families like you would have with your children, grandchildren, and great-grandchildren to look after you. We learned very early the importance of integrating groups together. If you look at the structure of Gay relationships, what some people would perceive as strange, such as, "We don't know why there are three guys living over there together. What are they doing?" Many times we've taken them in, because they need help.

During the AIDS crisis no one would help us. My other half's best friend was one of the first doctors who sent in blood samples. We knew about it when it was still called "GRID." I started working with people before there was even a name for it, because no one else would. We lived in our own community and we started raising money. We started the *Gay Men's Health Crisis.* We started the *AIDS Project Los Angeles.* We got together because no one would do it. So we built the models of incredible things for doing volunteer work, for reaching out and helping others. We also did *Angel Food,* which is a meals-on-wheels sort of thing. So you look at some of those support structures that we have built by ourselves within our community, because we had no where else to go. There is a group called the Rainbow Project, which is a support group for gay seniors, because where do they go? You can't put them into a rest home. So we take care of them. We take care of our own. One of the reasons that you don't see them is because we're taking care of them. You know, we bring them into our homes, those of us who have the capacity to do that. I think that the straight society could really learn some valuable lessons on family dynamics. On treating the aged well.

I don't know any straight old person in the world who doesn't have a Gay friend. You go to San Francisco and they talk about the dreaded Castro District. If you go walk around there, it's Gays and old people, because the Gay people will take care of the old people there. It's one of the safest places for old people to be in the city. They flock to get into places in that area because the Gay people look after them and we always have.

We also have managed to build equality into our relationships and very comfortably split roles. So where you are dealing with the husband-and-wife concept we've had no rules. We get to make our rules up. So I always laugh when people ask me if I like to stay home. I say, "Yes, I can paint your house. I can build it. I can remodel it. I can make you a dress at the same time, do your hair, and cook dinner." I mean I don't have a problem with that. So we as gay people are allowed to be in touch with all aspects. My masculinity is not affected by the fact that I can sew your drapes. Whereas the straight male out there goes, "Not a chance. I'm not going near a sewing machine." I'm saying, "Why?"

Author: You know, you should write two books. You should write one for the Seventh Day Adventists. You could lay out the structure for the very decent, very wonderful Gay relationships so you could be a teacher to your church. Then you have a different aspect of this wonderful organization that is outreaching to your ministers and educators. If you were to put that in a book it could be a great teaching tool. Then you should write another book for young Gay couples. Just think of all the young Gay couples who need counseling, who don't know how they are going to live a normal life.

Allen: Actually, within our group, at our camp meetings, one of the traditional things that we have done is use the couples within our organization to educate or inform the younger people.

So a lot of times we will put on a Seminar so that the younger kids can dialogue with those of us who have been in long term relationships. They can ask us questions. Whether they are in a new relationship, or if they are just newly "out" and they are not sure what to do. We also have a new politically correct hymnal because we have both gays and lesbians within our organization. We had to deal with these issues a few years ago. So we came up with, and wrote ourselves, a hymnal. We took music that we liked, that had been traditionally used within the church, and we wrote it so that we always refer to God as GOD, never as HIM. We have always used The Heavenly Being, and that is pretty common within a lot of the Gay Church groups. I prefer to see religion dealt with on a more matriarchal basis.

Author: I think you are thinking of the mother image. Mom is the one who kisses the hurts and rocks the baby and loves the family. But you know Jesus did not ask us to call on His Father in a stern Image. He told us to call Him ABBA, which translates as Daddy. The kind of a Daddy that you could climb up in His Lap, because you are His own child. I know that a lot of fundamentalist religions prefer that old hell-fire-damnation approach. They hold forth this Image of God as this punisher.

Allen: I'm sure that initially The Father was meant to be a much more Paternal Being, but I see Patriarchal as being domineering and rigid. You always see Him done in the big beard, and the white hair, and the flowing robes, and the frown; the wizened sort of person who is very wise. So I tend to be one of those who really like the mother image. I would like to go back if I had a time machine. I would have loved to have seen what the real Jesus looked like. I have always been intrigued. I see Him as any man, in any century, who has charisma. Martin Luther King, Kennedy, Gandhi; I mean these people had a thing that they just radiate. I see Jesus as that kind of a figure. If you put that kind of figure in that context, a first century man, I would really be intrigued to see the type of individual that He was. I love the words that are attributed to Him. He must have been incredibly simple and so wonderful in His own simplicity that you couldn't help but love Him. I would love to go back and meet him, just to see what He must have been like. He must have been absolutely astounding.

Here is another little piece of my philosophy over a number of years that people always feel when they ask about Gay people and what use are they? We're just pariahs to the world. We are always accused of collecting everything, and we learn all this stuff. We collect antiques, and I've thought that one of the reasons we always do that is when the big apocalypse comes and the dark ages set in again we'll be the ones with the knowledge. We will bring it back to the world, with all of the antiques and the books and the things. Maybe that is our place in life, maybe that's our role.

Author: I think God does have a role for you because He created you.

Allen: Like the monks who kept the books during the Dark Ages and brought art and things back to the world after the Dark Ages. Maybe that's our role down the line. Gather the information and then when the world needs it again, we will have it for them.

Author: The most important thing to remember about God, the most important thing of all, is that He loves you.

Allen: Well, that must be true or else they would have gotten rid of us a long time ago.

Chapter Twenty

Davi

Q: At what age did you first realize that you were gay?
A: I realized I was gay or different as far back as I can remember, around four or five years of age.

Q: What grade were you in?
A: I was in pre-school or kindergarten.

Q: What did you think about it?
A: I knew that I just felt different. I didn't really understand or know what it all meant. It was just that I liked girls and would develop crushes on them. My boyfriends were my buddies, my friends. I felt like one of them only because I shared their attraction to females.

Q: How did you cope with it?
A: It didn't cause a problem.

Q: How did you handle yourself about the boy-girl issue?
A: At that young age the boy-girl issue didn't matter. As I got older and I began to realize what all of this would entail, it became more difficult. I did a lot of pretending. I tried to fit in and be like the other girls. I would say I liked certain boys. I would even go so far as to go steady. But I never had the same attraction for boys as I did for girls. It just didn't ever "feel right."

Q: How did you cope with the situation?
A: I didn't have a problem because I did not come out of the closet.

Q: What kinds of toys did you play with?
A: I did play some with dolls. I also played with army men, games, race car sets, and marbles.

Q: What kinds of games did you play?

A: I played outdoors a lot. I rode bikes. I liked building tree houses and forts. I enjoyed playing army or Cowboys and Indians.

Q: How did the other kids and teachers treat you?

A: They didn't treat me any differently than anyone else because I never admitted to anyone that I was gay.

Q: How old were you when you finally came out?

A: I was thirty-five years old.

Q: Who was the first person that you were able to tell?

A: I first came out to a friend.

Q: When did you tell your parents?

A: I told my mom also when I was thirty-five. But I think that she had always suspected it.

Q: How did she take it?

A: My mom said that I had to pick between her and my girl-friend. If I didn't pick her, she would walk out of my life forever. She tried to lay a guilt trip on me about what I was doing to my son. I picked my girlfriend. My mom left, but returned shortly with tears in her eyes. She said she couldn't go through with it. She said that she would give things a try.

Q: How did your siblings treat you before they found out?

A: I am an only child. My other relatives haven't really treated me any differently than they treated me before I came out.

Q: Do you have anything special to tell, or share?

A: Just that I felt a tremendous burden was lifted from my shoulders after coming out. Not so much to others, but truly admitting it to myself. I did not have to live a lie anymore. I get frustrated with people and their closed narrow ideas about homosexuality. I know who and what I am. And I am not ashamed of it anymore.

Q: How does your family treat you now, since you are grown?

A: Basically the same, even though most of them believe this is a sin and perverted.

Q: How do your co-workers treat you on the job?

A: I am a professional in the nursing field and they are very accepting.

Q: Are you in a permanent relationship?

A: Yes.

Q: Do you want children?

A: I have a thirteen year old son. I had always wanted children. I had him when I was trying to fit the mold my family and society expected of me.

Q: Are you religious?

A: Not very... I do believe that there is a higher power. However, I do not believe that a person has to belong to a certain cult. There are certain moral laws that a person needs to live by.

Q: How are you coping with life in a straight society?

A: I am doing just fine.

Q: Have you had any special problems?

A: Not really.

Q: Is there something that you would like to say to the rest of the world?

A: Only that each person is an individual and should be judged as such. Each of us has our own story and set of circumstances that make us what we are. I personally believe that homosexuality is a pre-determined genetic trait. I believe that each person deals with it differently, and at different ages. I don't think that the Bible actually says anything specifically about homosexuals. Organized religion works on fear and guilt. They seem to work on hating certain groups and make homosexuals a prime target. On the whole, homosexuals are no different than any straight person. Just as there are deviants of every kind with heterosexuals, it doesn't mean that all straight people are deviants. The same thing is true with us. Don't compare us to pedophiles or murderers. We have families. We hold jobs. We own homes. We like to have fun. You may not agree with me or even understand me. That's fine. Just don't try to make me feel guilty or sinful for who I am.

Chapter Twenty-One

R. Jay

The first time that I realized that I was gay was as far back as I can remember. I was always looking at, and I had a certain attraction to, other men but I just took it for granted. I didn't think I was any different from anybody else. The earliest I can remember is about three years of age. When I went into elementary school, I was hanging around with the girls more. I was more feminine. I was playing jacks. I wasn't playing sports. But! I didn't think I was any different from anyone else until I was in junior high. When I was in seventh grade the kids started to realize things, and started deciding who was different and who is an outcast. It was then that I realized that there was something different about me, and that I had gay tendencies. It was when I put an exact label on it, and so did everybody else. So at that age I became like the outcast, the nerd, the geek. I was different because I didn't like playing sports. I was a sissy. I was called names. I was picked on. It got to the point that by the eighth grade, right before graduation, I remember I would cry. I remember crying that, if only I could be popular and I could be accepted, that's all I wanted. When I got to high school it was kind of scary at first because I thought it was going be the same thing only intensified. In actuality I found a group of friends, a little niche, and got myself established where things really didn't matter.

Now jumping back to when I was three years old, the things I remember were that my father was a body-builder, and he had a lot of body-building magazines, and I loved looking at those magazines. Not, of course, with a sexual desire, but still with a fondness. I was always looking at the male physique with a certain fondness.

I was always doing the things that girls did. I remember having a conversation once with my grandmother. I said, "I wish I was a girl. Girls are neater. I wish I was one." We had this big long conversation about it. She said, "No, you don't, you should be glad to be who you are." I said, "No, I really do wish I was a girl." They have pictures of me before I can remember, dressing up in my grandmothers wigs and dresses, and running out into the middle of company. I was always jumping out, all done up with pearls and everything. Of course, now I don't wish that I was a girl. I don't now, but I did then. Question: If you could start all over again, would you be a girl if you could? My answer is, "No."

That would change who I am as a person. I've gone through a lot of mistakes. I've had a lot of bad encounters in all sections of my life. I wouldn't change those. Because if I did, I wouldn't have learned the lessons that I have learned. I wouldn't have developed into the person that I am today. I don't want to alter that person. I think it's an acceptance thing, to be proud of who you are as a person. I don't wish to be anyone else. I'm happy being who I am. It is true that if I were a heterosexual it would have been an easier life to live. It would not have been as hard going through those stages. That's the same with a black person. They have it harder than a white. But if you asked them if they would start over and be white, most of them would say, "No." Because that would change who they are. The dressing up for me, and the performing, is exactly that. I love dressing up to perform. I love the art of illusion. I like the art of not looking like who you are, just in an acting sense. I've done that for fun. For the sake of hamming it up and acting, because I knew I could do it. It's nice to know that I can do it.

I'm in something now, and yes, I do dress up. It's a comedy troop. It's not trying to look like a girl. I do it because of the comedy factor. I'm not trying to impersonate something that I'm not. There is a difference. So now, even if I do dress up, it was always for the acting part of me, the entertaining part of me. It is not because I want to be a girl.

High school was very interesting because I went there in the mid-1980's. We came into an era that was called "Neuro." It was Neuro music when Duran Duran was big. The androgynous theme became very big. That was with makeup and with cross dressing clothes. Not so much wearing dresses, but unisex clothing. These were things that men and women would both wear. So, that made for a very interesting high school experience. That was the perfect time to "come out" if you were gay because, all of a sudden, it gave you an excuse. And then after about a year, that fad kind of went away. That was the time that I, and a lot of my peers, "came out." It was a helpful time era as far as "coming out." So when I did come out, I didn't get hated. I wasn't discriminated against. I didn't get really hate mail, except for those who never liked me in the first place. That didn't matter. I already had a group of friends who accepted me. If anything, I felt like I was more myself. I didn't have to hide anything, with the exception of my "at home" life, you know. At least at school I got to be exactly who I was, and nobody thought any differently of me. They didn't see me with a big label on my head. They just saw me as myself.

Unfortunately, with my parents, it was a different story. My parents split up when I was ten years old. I was raised by my father because he was the responsible one. My mother left on a little whim of frivolity, and so I was left with the responsible, religious-minded parent. Which was very interesting, because he has a hard time dealing with reality. He's one of those people who, unfortunately, if he doesn't see it, it doesn't exist. If it's not actually placed in front of his face, and you say here it is, he doesn't have to deal with it. I guess that he saw that his older son was effeminate. I guess that since I was born, he has seen those things. But! He chose to ignore it.

The way that he found out "Really for Certain" was an unfortunate event. When I became a teenager, I became very rebellious. I wanted to do my own thing. I was sneaking out at night. I would go off with my friends... Party... Then sneak back through the window. I was experimenting with alcohol. By this time I was sixteen years old. Well, one night I was experimenting with tequila with my friends and I got really drunk and everything got very fuzzy. All I remember is that my friends did manage to drop me off in the front yard of my own house. Then there is a lapse of time. All I remember next was that I was in the car with some Latino man who was maybe three years older than me. We were chatting and making out in this car. He wants to drive away and go off with me and then I realize, this is not my car. Then he says, "This is not my car either." So we jumped out of there really quick. He has this ice chest full of beer, and he says, "Let's go into your room." So I tried crawling through my window. He crawls through also. I grab the ice chest. It falls. It crashes. I'm soaked. The beer gets all over me. I put on a bathrobe. By this time my father knocks on the door, and I hadn't had time to totally change. So I answer the door with a bathrobe on and a strange Latino man standing in my room and beer. My father just flipped.

He wants to know what's going on. I make up some story that he's a friend of a friend who has no place to sleep tonight. I'm letting him stay the night and he was going to leave in the morning. I've known him for a long time — blah, blah, blah — trying to cushion it over. He tells the guy to leave. My father is beside himself, and we get into this argument. He calls me a fag — for the first time — because he doesn't believe any of this. Which leads to me going off on a big temper-tantrum and actually challenging my father, who is a body-builder. I just started screaming, and I actually lunged at him. He's doing all he can to force me off. By this time the guy is gone, and we get in this big fight. He's screaming things at me. You're just a homosexual. I said, "You'll never see me again as of the morning. I'll pack up my bags and I'll be gone." I'm just screaming and throwing the biggest tantrum. Then I can't see him or hear him so I calm down for a minute. I go into the hallway to see where he is. I can't find him. I go into the bathroom of his bedroom. He's curled up in a ball by the toilet, sobbing like a baby. That's the worst sight I've ever seen in my entire life. That's an image that will never be wiped from my memory. It's one that I truly regret to this day. Of course, I stopped crying the minute I saw this. I tried comforting him. I said, "I'm sorry dad, I'm sorry about all of this, I didn't mean any of this." He just told me to go to bed.

The next morning I didn't know how I was going to approach him. He said, "Just forget it. It never happened." He basically did forget it, like it never happened. The only other time I was confronted by him was when I was eighteen years old. By this time I'm hanging out with my peers, in front of the gay bars on the weekend. A man at his office comes up to him and says, "I have something to tell you. It's your son R. Jay. He's gay! He hangs out in front of the gay bars, with his friends."

He came up to me after about three days of going through personal turmoil. For those three days I remember him not looking me in the eye. He would avoid me. He was ashamed. I couldn't for the life of me figure out why. Finally, on the third day, I grabbed him and said, "Dad you have got to talk to me. What is going on? I can't take this. Let's just go talk. If you're having problems, you know I have always been there for you." He used to be able to tell me about his first wife, and I would listen. So we go out on the front steps of our house and he sits down. The first words he says to me are, "I don't think your and my relationship will ever be the same, after this conversation. I have heard from a reliable source that you are gay and that you hang out in front of the gay bar."

I've always been good at lying to my father and helping him to be deceived. For the first time I've actually seen that look in his eyes saying, "Make up one of your stories. Lie to me. Tell me something else to pass me through this." For the first time ever I decided, "Not this time." I'm going to be totally truthful. I'm going to tell you the truth. I said, "It's true. I'm Gay and, yes, I have been there." I saw all the pain and all of the realization and everything just flash in front of his eyes and just hit his heart. He was right, because for the first time I was truthful, and from that point on our relationship has never been the same. He's uncomfortable when I'm around. He acts like he doesn't know quite how to deal with me. You can see the edginess whenever I am around. So now I'm twenty-six years old. This happened when I was eighteen.

Soon after that incident, I was excommunicated from my religion, which is Jehovah's Witness. They're very strict, they have very set rules. I went to the elder at my father's request. He said you can't keep this a secret. You have to let them know. It was a very private meeting, between myself and three elders.

We went over the scriptures. Basically their opinion is: Your sexual tendencies are not the problem. You can't control that. What you can control is whether you actually sleep with someone or not. They read a scripture for me. As they interpret it one of the apostles said that he used to pummel his body daily to fight the urges of the flesh. They brought up that scripture to show what he went through. So all they asked is that I abstain. So after three long meetings and discussions they couldn't decide whether or not they should excommunicate me. Their final opinion after the third meeting was that they would excommunicate me. If I am truly repentant, I will still come to the meetings, even though no one could speak to me. You are actually an outcast! If you can make it through that, and still stick with it, and come to the meetings, then we will see that you are truly repentant. You can be reinstated to the religion.

Soon after that incident of my being excommunicated, they announced it. I wasn't there. I stayed home. For some reason I felt like a weight had been lifted off my shoulders. I felt almost free. Soon after that my father and I got into another argument, about me sneaking off for the weekend. He said, "I bet you went to West Hollywood and you were hanging out with the boys." We got into a big fight. He said he wanted me out. I was out the next day. He gave me a week, and I got out the next day.

I lived with my best friend who I have known now for the last ten years. He and I have ended up moving in together, off and on. We have been like best friends or like brothers, not sexually. Most people have the opinion that if two homosexuals are friends that they are sleeping together. I am here to say that is just not true. It's ridiculous, but people think that way. People tend to pigeonhole homosexuals, like they are all the same. They all sleep around and it is all a sexual thing with them. It's not true. You have homosexuals who have many different faces and personalities, just like you have in the heterosexual community. You have those who are promiscuous. Then you have homosexuals who have been faithful for years. I have friends who have been together for eighteen years. They wouldn't dream of sleeping with anybody else. They are monogamous.

So! That is what happened between my father and myself. Now that I am twenty-six, he is finding it a little bit easier. He doesn't have to see me except on holidays and special occasions. Recently I went down to see my grandmother. She has always been able to accept me because she has always seen me as just one thing: her grandson. That's who I am. She never claims to understand it. But she doesn't push me out as well. The last time I was there, my dad called me up and made a special effort to spend time together. He wanted to see me, and we spent a really nice time together. So I think as the years roll by that he is learning that I'm just R. Jay... Myself... It's kind of unfortunate that his best memories of me are of a rebellious teenager who also happened to be homosexual. That's kind of sad.

My mother on the other hand didn't have much of a chance to raise me after I was ten years old. She didn't get to see me all that often. I was twenty years old when we got back together. She came to live with me for about four days. She was on a vacation kind of thing. I let her know then. I just came out and told her. She had the typical mothers' response. She said, "I've always known; I've always thought that." Then I proceeded to tell her something that I have never told anyone with the exception of my father. Two of her cousins, from her side of the family, molested me when I was a child. One was male and started when I was six years old. The other one was female; she started when I was about seven years old.

There is an opinion that some people become gay because of a traumatic situation that happened in their childhood. I, for one, can say I have had that type of situation happen to me. It is an interesting situation because I was molested by both sexes. I've come across many straight guys who have been molested by other men and are still straight. So I don't think that is a premise for anything. I was molested by both a guy and a girl. At separate times. During the same span of my life. So it could have influenced me either way. But I still have the same preferences that I always had. It wasn't until I was ten years old that I finally was able to stand up to that cousin who was molesting me. He was doing the typical lies. Like if you tell anybody, your parents will hate you. All the things to manipulate me and to make me do these things against my will. Finally, when I was ten years old, I said, "Look, if you touch me again I'm going to go shout it out to your father, your mother and everybody in the middle of that living room. I'll let everyone know. You can't fool me anymore. You touch me and you're history." When I was ten, I finally had the strength to do that.

If it wasn't me that it happened to it would have happened to my brother, who was straight. I'm kind of glad that it did work out that way. I was the stronger of the two. My brother, unfortunately, has the exact kind of mental being as my father. He can't deal with trauma like that. He just can't. So it happened to the stronger of the two souls. A lot of the things I did do, I did because my brother was in the next bed. I would rather have it happen to me than him. So in that way, I feel like I protected my younger brother.

When I was sixteen, I finally, voluntarily, decided to be with a girl. It was under the influence of alcohol. She persuaded me. Her goal was to try to switch me. This girl, I liked. She looked like a sixteen year old Marilyn Monroe. So we slept together. I was able to function and I was not repulsed. I was able to make it all the way through the sexual experience. Since that instance I have done it again with a different girl. But I will tell you that I personally have never orgasmed with a female. Never. I could get myself to concentrate and be functional and go through the actions without fail, but I could never orgasm.

On a different subject, I haven't had a problem in the work place. Of course, I live in Los Angeles, but I have also lived in a small town where I was raised. Of all the jobs I've had recently, there's been no problem. I don't come out and tell people right off the bat that I am homosexual. If someone is curious and they want to know, I will tell them. I'm open enough that I won't lie about it. I have never had a problem at the job I work at now, nor the two jobs that I worked at before. There has always been great acceptance. I'm always one of the most liked employees in the entire place. I'm the one with the personality, the sense of humor. I can always make people laugh. I have never had a heterosexual change their mind about liking me as a friend because they found out. Currently I work with a lot of heterosexuals. They all take me just as anyone else. From eighteen years old on I made friends with homosexuals who associated with other homosexuals, which was a way of being sheltered away from the heterosexual world. I didn't go to the bars that they went to. I didn't hang out with them at all. So the fact that I, all of a sudden, have all of these heterosexual people that I work with liking me and wanting me to come to their parties, to their bars, and to hang out with them, even though they know. They have no problem with it.

It's kind of a new experience for me. I'm glad. I'm realizing now that I'm not having those prejudices. I did previously. I didn't want to go where "they" were. Now I'm finding out that I can be comfortable no matter where I am because they are accepting of me. I'm at the point now where I can do that.

Some day I hope to be able to meet someone and settle down and stay in a committed relationship. Unfortunately, I've never had a serious monogamous relationship in my entire life. I've always been single. And believe me there's a great desire to find the right person and settle down. Yes, I hope for two things. I want to find the right person and have a serious monogamous relationship that I can settle down with and grow old with. I'm praying for that. I do hope and pray that I find someone.

I know you're going to ask this and yes, I do want to have children. I do realize that is involving a woman in the picture. That's the way I would want it. If I like this woman enough where I would want her to be the mother of the child I was rais-ing, then I want it to be a team effort. I want a woman who would go in on a partnership, and raise the child as a partnership and have two separate homes. I would want to make sure that it was not only myself, but another woman who loved this child and raised it. I would want it to be similar to a divorce type part-nership where both parents not only have equal visitation rights but kind of an even partnership. Just living in two separate homes. It's hard to find an open-minded woman who is willing do that. I want the child to have the best and I want the child to have a mother and a father. I do think I would make a perfect father. My orientation is not going to play into raising the child. This will be my flesh and blood. I guess I do kind of have that father pride, trying to carry on the family name. Adopting is great but I don't want to adopt. I want to know it came from me. When I'm ready to settle down and be responsible and have everything situated right I will be searching for that.

The reason I am doing this interview is that I think I'm going to reach a group of people who really need to hear it. Even though I was not raised a Catholic Christian, I was still raised with a conservative family. I just want them to know homosexuality is not something that as a parent you should feel is your fault. It is not something that is wrong, that is like a problem. You don't have to spend your time going through pain and pointing a finger and trying to figure out what went wrong. It's an extra situation. It's an extra factor in your life. Just open your eyes and open your heart. The best possible thing you can do is be open, verbally and emotionally, with the people that you know and love. Remember that person is your son, your daughter, your brother, your sister. That is the person that you loved before you found out, and it's still the same person after you found out. Nothing has changed. Absolutely nothing in the entire world has changed, except for some information that has been given to you. So you take that information and all of that love, and all of the care that you have always had, and use it. Don't be afraid to question, don't be afraid to ask, and don't be afraid to share. That would be the biggest help that any person could possibly have. I do believe there is a God. I have chosen not to go back to the religion that I was raised on. Not because I don't believe there is a God. I found it hard to believe in some of the ways that they have taught. Here are some of the things I do believe in.

For instance they say God is a loving God. God is a generous God.

God can understand a situation in a human being tenfold more than any human being can understand another. He knows our heart and He knows who we are. How can you expect an understanding and a loving God to be any less than a human? He understands more, and He knows more, and He loves more. So if a human can understand the homosexual situation, and understand it for what it is, how can you expect God not to? So I have chosen not to follow any certain denomination. Because they are all in one way or another flawed. Men go through history, tampering with it in their own way, forcing their own personal views in certain areas where they think it needs to be. So I stay just as close to God as I can, through a personal relationship, through prayer and through a one-on-one basis. I feel as long as I'm honest, I can talk to him through prayer and do my best throughout my life.

That's the best that I can do with everything that I have learned in my life. Anytime anyone shuts me out and doesn't want to listen or love or understand that's always hurtful. Every person in this entire world has had somebody hurt them. Everybody, it's just a fact of life. It doesn't matter who you are. That is a growing experience, and that is a learning experience. Anybody who has gone through a life and hasn't had anybody hurt them or disappoint them isn't going to grow and learn very much. So yes, people have hurt me. But I learn from it, I think about it, and I grow from it. Any time anyone doesn't want to open up, or to understand, and just keep themselves closed, that does hurt me. I think that's kind of sad. Especially for that person.

CHAPTER TWENTY-TWO

JOCELYN MARIE

Author: How old were you when you first discovered that there was a difference in the way that you felt about boys?

Jocelyn: When I was younger I had crushes on girls. I was in about third grade. I had crushes on older girls in upper classes. But I didn't think anything of it at the time. I always had girls that I looked up to and thought were pretty. I never thought anything of it until I met Susan when I was twenty. I'm twenty-three now.

Author: When you were in third grade and you were having crushes on girls, what did you think? Did you tell anyone?

Jocelyn: I never said anything to anybody because I didn't know if it was normal. I thought, "What if someone thinks I'm crazy?" I was really quiet. I didn't say anything very much at all. I didn't even tell my mom. I didn't tell anyone. I just kind of kept it to myself.

Author: When you were that age, did you ever have a crush on a boy?

Jocelyn: Yeah, but they were different kinds of crushes. It was like everybody liked guys. It was like, I've got a crush on this guy because he's cute. They were all really mean people in my school. I didn't like that.

Author: Do you ever think that if you ever met a really nice guy who was sensitive and kind, that you could ever have a relationship with him?

Jocelyn: Yeah, I could easily. But it was different with Susan. I had boyfriends, but at some time in my relationship they would cheat on me, or treat me like garbage. Or they would just leave me. I don't know why. My dad left when I was fifteen. From that day forward, every guy in my life left at some point. When I met Susan, I was at that point where I had just gotten out of a relationship with a guy who was really mean to me. I was having so many troubles with guys, I never wanted to go near them again.

It was really weird, the way we met. I had this friend, Sunshine, who I was hanging out with. I really didn't get along with a lot of girls. Sunshine said that she was going to bring a couple of friends to *Fuzzies,* this place where we play pool. When Susan walked in, I felt like "WOW," I want to be her best friend. I looked at her and I thought, "Oh my God, she's incredible. I have to be friends with her. I have to be something with her." She had thigh high Doc Martens on, and a little velvet dress and garters. Her hair had been shaved and it was growing out; the part that had been shaved was about 4 inches. The long part was about to the middle of her back. It was three different colors: brown, red and black. She had this black makeup that comes out to here on her eyes, like Susie and The Banshees. I saw her and I thought, "I have to talk to her." Then I made her be my friend. I pursued it to such an extent that she had to be my friend. About six months into our friendship, we decided that we wanted to be together. She was always interested in homosexuality, but she never had a friend that she could tell about it. We used to talk about it all the time. She said that she wanted to be together and we were together for two and a half years. I had never felt like that. From the moment I saw her, I just knew that I had to be something to her. I had to be part of her life. She is an incredible person.

Then for a month and a half I didn't see her because I was still with this guy. He totally abused me. He was a really awful person. I remember I broke up with him one time, and it was two weeks before I broke up with him for the final time. She was the only friend who stuck by me through that relationship. She said, "If this is what makes you happy, and this is what you want, then I'm behind you 100%." She said that she didn't like him and she knew she wouldn't get to see me. But she would have rather me be happy, if that is what I wanted, than to get what she wanted, which was to be with me. It took me two weeks to figure out that I wanted to be with this person. I had a nervous breakdown because of my relationship with him. He had mentally abused me so badly I was like a basket case. It was Valentine's Day. Susan took me out so I wouldn't have to be at the house. When I got home that evening, there was a big box all wrapped and tied up with a big bow, and a balloon on it that said, "Sorry," from Todd. I thought he was apologizing because he was sorry for being a jerk all this time. So I opened it up and there was a card and a big letter inside. It said, "I'm sorry that I ever thought you were a person." There was this long letter saying how much he hated me; that nothing between us ever mattered. All of the things I ever gave him he gave back to me. Also there was this key chain that said, "You were put on this earth to make my life miserable." That's what he thought I was to him and I just freaked.

Susan was right there. I went outside where we had a stucco wall by the back driveway. I started banging my hands into it, and my hands were all bloody, and I started banging my head. And Susan, she stopped me. If it wasn't for her I think I would have gone crazy. I think that's when it started. When I just totally fell for her. She was always there and she was the strongest person. She was the first person whoever showed me what love was. Because my family is really not loving. Every boyfriend I ever had treated me like garbage. I never knew what it was like to be loved. She loved me unconditionally. No matter what I did, no matter what I said, it didn't matter and she wouldn't go away.

Like we would fight and I would try to make her go. I would push her away and say to her, "I just want you to go away." And she would say, "Why don't you get it through your head that I'm not leaving." Finally I got it through my head. She was the best thing that ever happened to me.

Author: When you were growing up, what kind of toys did you play with?

Jocelyn: I was a tomboy. I played football. I played with my brother. I played with G.I. Joes. I had Barbies, and I played with them when my friends came over. But I didn't play with them when I was by myself. When I was by myself, I played with trucks. I played football with my brother in the street, and soccer, and I played basketball. I wore my hair up in a ponytail and I wore a baseball cap. I wore jeans and zip tennis shoes, a white tee shirt, and a black leather jacket. I wanted to be Fonzie. He was cool. That's what I was like. I was a tomboy.

Author: How did you get along with the other kids in school?

Jocelyn: I didn't. The first three years I was fine, until I got to third grade. I don't know what happened. I'm like a really bubbly person. I like to have fun and I like to do things. I like to be happy all the time. And this girl, she was the principal's daughter, and maybe I was taking too much attention away from her. She kind of made the whole school hate me. So I didn't have any friends. I got beat up almost every single day. So I didn't get along with anybody really. I tried but they didn't like me. I pretty much didn't have any friends at school. I hung out with kids who were younger than me. I went to a private school, and I kicked rocks around during recess. I would never fight back.

Author: How old were you when you first came out?

Jocelyn: I came out at twenty with Susan. Actually Susan and I just came out to everybody. I didn't tell my mother. I didn't tell her until a couple years later. Susan and I were going to get married. We were supposed to get married this year, over spring break. Unfortunately, we broke up. When we were getting close to getting married, then I had to tell my mom. Surprise! Before that we didn't keep it a secret, but we didn't go out and make it a public thing. You could tell we were together. Both of us were so happy to be together. We felt like, why would anybody care, because it's a joy for us. If they didn't like it that's too bad, because we didn't care what they think. We didn't make it like a thing.

Author: You said you were twenty when you first came out. Did you have a mom and a dad and did you talk to both of them?

Jocelyn: No, I've never told my father. My dad wouldn't care. He wouldn't say anything. It's hard to talk to my dad. I really don't like to talk to my mother either. We really don't have a close relationship. Either one of us. My dad is very much a stickler about everything. If it doesn't pertain to my grades, my car, or a job, he doesn't want to know anything about it. He doesn't want to know about my private life. He doesn't want to know what I do.

Author: How did your mom take it?

Jocelyn: She freaked out. She screamed. She raved. She said, "When did you decide that you were gay." She yelled for a couple of days. Then she just kind of forgot about it. She's still in denial about it. Since Susan and I broke up, I haven't had another girlfriend, so I think she's just gone and forgotten about it. And I've let her. Cause I don't want her yelling anymore. I'm done. The yelling was enough. She just kind of swept it under the carpet. She acted like it didn't happen, because that's what she does with everything. Every once in a while, when she gets angry, she will bring up some little thing. But she doesn't usually say anything. She doesn't treat me any differently. We don't get along. We never did. It's not going to change now.

Author: Do you have any brothers and sisters? Do you still get along?

Jocelyn: My oldest sister took it nonchalantly. My other sister had done the same thing. She called it her experimental stage, she was living with a woman for a year. She felt totally comfortable with it. I never told my brother.

Author: How would he take it?

Jocelyn: He would beat the crap out of me. Like he does for anything else. So no, my brother is not ever going to know. My brother is right-wing, conservative Republican. He believes that this is the way that God made you, and this is the way you should be. He is really *really* a stickler. He thinks one opinion, and he thinks that is the opinion that everyone should have on everything. My brother is just that way. My dad's not like that, he's wishy-washy. He doesn't care. He doesn't bother talking about anything. My mom, she's just opinionated about everything. She's very prejudiced. I would like to tell my mom, "It's not so bad." She doesn't have to sweep everything under the carpet, like it's kind of messy. She's going to have to get over it and deal with life. And my dad, there's nothing to say to my dad, he's funny. I like my dad to a certain extent. My brother, he has to stop being opinionated, and start accepting other people for who they are and what they are. One nephew is eight years old, and I think he is too young to understand. My other nephew is fifteen and I raised him. So he understands everything.

Author: Have you ever been treated any differently in the work place?

Jocelyn: When they first found out about me, a lot of people changed their attitude toward me. They were not as friendly.

There were a lot of girls that worked there, and they felt uncomfortable around me. They thought that I was going to go for them. I wanted to tell them, "I don't want you."

Author: I know you have recently broken up but would you like to someday be in a permanent relationship?

Jocelyn: Yes I would, but it's kind of hard for me to think about it because Susan and I have just recently broken up. We broke up in March. Then we hung out for a while, around her birthday, which is in May. That really hurt me because I knew we couldn't see each other anymore. She was crying all of the time, every time we saw each other. When she left, she moved to Oregon. She cried on my shoulder and she told me that she loved me.

Author: It's obvious that you two love each other. What happened to your relationship? Why did you break up?

Jocelyn: One of the reasons was that Susan had disappeared for three months to Oregon. She didn't call anybody and she was doing drugs. I don't believe in doing that anymore. We used to do that when we first started going out. But I quit. I don't want anything more to do with it. She went away, and when she came back, she was a different person. She did things behind my back. She lied to me about things. She had never done that to me before.

Author: I get the feeling that you still love her.

Jocelyn: Oh, I still love her to death. I would give my right eye to go back to her again, but she's changed so much since she went totally into drugs. Her brain is gone. She's done ice. Do you know what ice is? It's a really strong crystal methamphetamine. She did heroin a couple of times.

She did Acid and Ecstacy. I was talking to her and she was like "out there" someplace. You can't relate to a person when they're like that. I couldn't. I just left. I cried. She's the person who gave me strength. The person who changed the way that I look at myself, the way I think about myself. The person that had been my tower of strength basically. She kept me up on my feet and pushed me to be in school. She pushed me to be in a job. She pushed me to be somebody, and to get my life together. To see her like that just broke my heart.

Author: Do you want to settle down and have kids someday?

Jocelyn: Yeah, I like kids. I have to get a guy somewhere... [She laughs]

Author: Do you consider yourself promiscuous?

Jocelyn: Not anymore. No.

Author: Are you religious? Do you believe in God?

Jocelyn: Yes, I do... [She laughs] That's a question and a half. You see, I was in a cult for three months. I got out of it, and it was scary. It was right after I broke up with Susan and they preyed on me because I was really down. They had me going around declaring loudly that, "This is the best thing that's ever happened to me."... *God this. God that...* Every single second of the day they had to know exactly where I was and who I was with. I couldn't tell them that I went to a movie with a friend. It got worse. When I quit, they would follow me. But aside from that, I do believe in God, but you see, now I'm terrified of death. I do believe that there is a heaven and a hell and it frightens me. After being in that cult. They brainwashed you. If you left them, you left God. You were going straight to the bad place. It's taking me so long to come to grips with this. I'm so terrified of death now, because of that, and I'm not sure now.

I have to get my feet back on the ground. I have to tell myself every day that Jesus loves me.

Author: Are you experiencing any rejection on the job now?

Jocelyn: In the job place. My boss does not know. I've been his nanny for his kids for several years. I have decided not to tell him since it would probably affect my relationship with him, and his family, and his children. I do not want that to happen. I'm the same person that I have been for the past four years. I haven't changed. So why bother saying anything. All it would do is cause problems for him and me. I really don't think that would be necessary. Other than that I'm very open about it and I'm open with my friends. One friend didn't speak to me for four months, but she came back. I've told my best friend. I'm straight up. I told her that I had a girl friend for two and a half years. Everyone who knew Susan and me knew we were a couple. No one had a problem with it. I think I have enough problems with my family to last me for about a hundred years.

Author: If you could say something to the world that you would like everyone to know about being gay what would you say?

Jocelyn: It's not that much different from being straight. It really isn't. You see, I've been both places. I can say that the relationship that I had with Susan was the best relationship that I ever had. You shouldn't judge things that you don't know anything about and haven't lived yourself. I think that everyone has their opinion about stuff. Until they have lived it, they don't have a right to have an opinion. I've lived it, so I have a right to have an opinion and it's the same. It was the same as a straight relationship as far as I was concerned. Susan understood how much I needed to be loved and where and how to love me without making me feel like I had to have sex with somebody. Most men think sex is the way you show love. Susan wasn't like that at all. She made me feel loved because she loved me, and not because she wanted to have sex. There is a very different stigma for a woman to be gay than it is for a guy. Men accept it like it's no big deal. But a guy's attitude about another guy is that it's gross. I mean where do they get the right to feel like that. I have arguments with them. I say if you think it's all right for girls to be together, then why isn't it OK for guys to be together. It's a double standard and that's not fair.

Author: Do you mean guys accept it for girls, but not in other guys?

Jocelyn: Yes, also girls accept it for guys to be together but not other girls.

Author: Would you like to invite your mother to a support group for families of Gays and Lesbians so that she would get a better understanding?

Jocelyn: I don't know if my mother would go. All of my life, from the day that I was born, my mom has let me go through everything by myself. Most of my friends will describe me as the strongest person that they ever met because I never had any mommy to go crying to.

When I got beat up at school my mom would say, "Just another year, just another year." It went that way until eighth grade. She never looks at anything in my life. She would probably have a fit about it, then she would ignore it. Then never say another word about it. Then, if I mentioned it, there would just be a huge fight. That's how my mom is; she doesn't look at anything. She puts blinders on and sees only what's in front of her. Then she doesn't even see *that,* because it's skewed by her own opinion. It's really hard to get along with her. She's really bitter. She's a very unhappy woman. She is not willing to accept anything that she considers out of the norm.

She's wonderful with my brother. They have a great relationship, because he's a boy. She treats my sisters like garbage. I'm the one that she treats the best, because I don't take any of her crap. If she yells at me, I yell right back. I don't let my mom hurt me. But she hurts my sister because my sister will take it.

I raised my nephew. He is the only one in my entire family that I consider myself close to. I raised him from a baby. My sister went into post-partum depression, and just never came out. She's never really been a mother. My nephew gave me the best compliment the other day. He was in the car with some friends and they said, "Jocelyn is not your mom," and he said, "Yes, she is. She's the closest thing I've ever had to a mom. My mom doesn't do anything for me. Jocelyn pays for my books, my school, my classes, my food, and my clothes. She makes sure that I'm OK every day." I raised him. He called me mom until he was four. He's my baby. I love him so much. He's 5'10" tall now, can you believe it? He was premature. He was two and a half pounds when he was born. He was an itty bitty teeny guy. He had a Mohawk because they had to shave his head to put IV's into his head. He was the most darling little baby. He was my life... He was my kid. I taught him how to walk. Every picture of him has me in it, or I took it. I have a whole photo album of just pictures of him. I have a big picture on my desk, and little ones around the room. I think of him as mine.

My family is a bunch of liars. My sister, his mom, is one of the biggest ones. I have never lied to him. If I tell him I'm going to get him something, he gets it. If I say he can't have something, then he can't have it. I stick to my word. He trusts me. She has never done that. She will tell him something and then she never does it. She goes back on her word. She told him he could stay with us. Then she moved out with a guy and changed her mind.

Now she tells him he has to move out with her. Another disappointment for him.

Author: There are many more stories out there. We are all so human, and we all have our comedies and tragedies. An ancient Indian saying goes, "You can't judge a man until you have walked a day in his moccasins." I hope these stories have given you an insight and helped you realize that these kids are no different than you or me, with the exception of who they are able to fall in love with.

NOTES — BIBLIOGRAPHY

1. "Homosexuality — The Test Case for Christian Sexual Ethics", James P. Hanigan, *Theological Inquiries-Studies in Contemporary Biblical and Theological Problems,* General Editor Lawrence Boadt, C.S.P. Paulist Press, New York, Mahwah-Chapter 1, pg. 25 (1988).
2. *Who Wrote The Bible?,* Richard Elliott Friedman, Harper and Row (1987).
3. *Reading The Old Testament, An Introduction,* Lawrence Boadt, Paulist Press (New York, 1984).
4. *Confraternity Edition of the Holy Bible of Christian Doctrine,* Good Counsel Publishing Co., Chicago, Illinois, (1961) Imprimatur: Walter A. Coggin O.S.B. Ph.D., D.D. Abbot-Ordinary, Diocese of Belmont Abbey, Nullius.
5. *Commentary on the Torah: Genesis,* Ramban (Nachmanides), trans. Charles Chavel (New York, 1971).
6. *The Torah: A Modern Commentary,* Union of American Hebrew Congregations (New York, 1981).
7. *Same-Sex Unions in Pre-Modern Europe,* John Boswell, Villard Books, (1994).
8. *The Church and the Homosexual,* John J. McNeill, Beacon Press (Boston, MA, 1976).

ABOUT THE AUTHOR

Jesse Davis was born of working class parents in the early years of the depression of the 1930's. Her father died of tuberculosis before her first birthday. Her mother remarried, and the family moved to Southern California where she continued her education in Catholic schools. Her studies at a secular college included accounting and psychology.

In the early years of her marriage, she worked with her husband in his building and land development business as a bookkeeper. After studying interior design, she took over the design work for the company.

All of her five children are independent, willful, opinionated, and high achievers. The first four are heterosexual. Three are engaged in the building business, while the fourth, who graduated *cum laude* from a major Catholic University, is a drummer in his own rock and roll band. The youngest is homosexual and is involved in acting, modeling and writing science fiction and fantasy.

In more recent years, she has taken up the study of the Old Testament. This has been invaluable in portions of this work. She has started a prayer group ministry for Catholic parents of gay and lesbian children. Many of these parents are confused and unhappy. Her interviews and correspondence with these parents form the basis for her next work.

Jesse has focused much of her time on volunteer work and community service and is a founding member of the South Counties Community Clinic. Her hobbies include traveling and photography.

INDEX